WHAT WONDROUS LOVE IS THIS

Great Hymns of Our Faith

BOOK 1:

O Worship the King

BOOK 2:

O Come, All Ye Faithful

BOOK 3:

What Wondrous Love Is This

Hymns of Wonder and Worship to Remember His Love

What Wondrous Love Is This

JONI EARECKSON TADA

JOHN MACARTHUR

ROBERT & BOBBIE WOLGEMUTH

CROSSWAY BOOKS • WHEATON, ILLINOIS

A DIVISION OF GOOD NEWS PUBLISHERS

Published by Crossway Books
A division of Good News Publishers
1300 Crescent Street
Wheaton, Illinois 60187

Design: Cindy Kiple

First printing: 2002

Printed in the United States of America

ISBN 1-58134-366-3 Book and CD set (sold only as a set)

LIBRARY OF CONGRESS CATALOGING-IN-PUBLICATION DATA
What wondrous love is this : hymns of wonder and worship to remember
his love / [compiled by] John MacArthur ... [et al.].
    p.   cm. — (Great hymns of our faith ; bk. 3)
  ISBN 1-58134-366-3 (alk. paper)
   1. Jesus Christ—Passion—Meditations. I. MacArthur, John, 1939-
II. Series.
BT431.3 .W43   2001
264'.23—dc21   2001008182
                                    CIP

15	14	13	12	11	10	09	08	07	06	05	04	03	02
15	14	13	12	11	10	9	8	7	6	5	4	3	2

With immense gratitude to Clayton Erb
who has served alongside me as Minister of Music for 23 years,
whose love of sound theology and beautiful music
has motivated him to fill our Worship Center and
our lives with great hymns.

JOHN MACARTHUR

———

To my sister, Jay Kay Tregenza.
For all the times our voices—soft as country down—
blended in harmony, making our praises to God
as sweet as the honeysuckle on our farm.

JONI EARECKSON TADA

———

To Dr. Raymond J. Gardner.
Bobbie's daddy, who always made sure his girls
had a corsage to go along with their Easter hats and white gloves.
To a gentle father, who tenderly paved the way
for this girl to love, trust, and confide in the man she married.

ROBERT & BOBBIE WOLGEMUTH

———

SPECIAL THANKS TO:

MR. JOHN DUNCAN
of TVP Studios, Greenville, SC,
Executive Producer of the musical recording
for *What Wondrous Love Is This.*

DR. PAUL PLEW
Chairman of the Department of Music
at The Master's College,
who directed the musical production.

THE STUDENTS OF THE MASTER'S CHORALE
who contributed their superb singing skills
and love for these hymns to the CD.

We are deeply grateful for the gifts of these friends
and accomplished professionals.

The publisher's share of income from the *What Wondrous Love Is This* compact disc is being donated by Good News Publishers/Crossway Books to Joni and Friends, the worldwide disability outreach of Joni Eareckson Tada. For more information about Joni and Friends, please write to Joni and Friends, Post Office Box 3333, Agoura Hills, California 91301 or call 818-707-5664 or go to the website—www.joniandfriends.org

TABLE OF CONTENTS

FOREWORD

Quite an unusual story lies behind the writing of the books in this series. But then we might expect as much because the authors—Joni Eareckson Tada, John MacArthur, and Robert and Bobbie Wolgemuth—are such extraordinary people!

In the broadest sense this book is the story of God's unfailing faithfulness, as told in the great hymns of the faith and in the stories that lie behind these hymns. Whether written in the midst of overwhelming tragedy or in moments of great joy, the hymns in the books in this series have profoundly touched the lives of Christians through the centuries—and they will do so again as these books are read.

But the immediate story behind this series starts (as many unusual stories do!) with our very dear friend Joni Eareckson Tada. Joni, as you know, broke her neck in a diving accident when she was seventeen years old, and she has lived as a quadriplegic for more than three decades ever since. But by God's grace and through Joni's perseverance, she lives a most extraordinary life—a life that above all else reflects the joy of the Lord. One of my favorite memories, in fact, is stopping with Joni in hotel lobbies to sing impromptu hymns of praise and worship—to the delight and sometimes wonder of other hotel guests.

The occasion that gave birth to this series of books and accompanying CDs, then, was *Joni's* idea—this time to sing "impromptu hymns" with Dr. John MacArthur at the Good News-Crossway 60th Anniversary Banquet, in the summer of 1998. The theme for the banquet was "Celebrating Sixty Years of God's Faithfulness," and both Joni and John MacArthur, Joni's pastor and close friend, were scheduled to speak. Joni and John checked with me first to be sure it was okay—and of course Joni doesn't take "no" for an answer! But it came as a complete surprise to everyone else when Joni invited John to join her on the platform to sing an "impromptu" duet of their favorite hymns.

Rarely have I seen an audience so deeply moved. As they listened to Joni sing the praises of God's faithfulness, it was a remarkable moment—a moment when we were all given a glimpse of God's glory.

Immediately after the banquet I started urging John and Joni to make a CD of hymns. And from there the ideas just kept growing. Joni invited her friends Robert and Bobbie Wolgemuth to join in since, as Joni noted, "We've sung together for years . . . over the telephone, in hotel lobbies, in restaurant parking lots, and they'd love to be part of this." And of course we'd need a book to go with the CD. But there are so many great hymns, we soon realized we'd really need *four* books!

All these ideas have come together in a most exciting way for each book so far. The recording studio was booked; John MacArthur brought Dr. Paul Plew and the highly acclaimed Chorale of The Master's College; and Joni, John, Robert, and Bobbie joined in singing some of the greatest hymns of all time. As Joni reflected after recording the CD for the first book, *O Worship the King*, "The adventure of singing together was pure delight. It was two solid days of worship and praise."

Now, several years after Joni "cooked up" her idea for a duet, her idea continues to come to life in the books in this series and in the CDs tucked into the back covers. It is our prayer that through these books and CDs you will also see a glimpse of God's glory and discover a deeper understanding of His faithfulness, and that you would join with Joni and John and Robert and Bobbie—and indeed the Church of our Lord Jesus Christ through the centuries—in singing the praises of our Lord and Savior.

"Christ the Lord is ris'n today," Alleluia!
Sons of men and angels say, Alleluia!
Raise your joys and triumphs high; Alleluia!
Sing ye heav'ns, and earth, reply. Alleluia!

Lane T. Dennis, Ph.D.
Publisher

INTRODUCTION

It's Easter!

Churches are packed. Little girls wearing hats and white gloves—too young to argue with their mothers over wardrobe issues—sit quietly on rock-hard pews. Little boys facing the same non-negotiable circumstances tug at their suit coats, do battle with their neckties, and shift in their seats.

After church families gather for a sumptuous dinner. And later neighborhoods are filled with the happy squeals of basket-toting children, looking for brightly colored plastic eggs hiding in bushes, among blooming daffodils, or in rain downspouts.

These scenes mark the celebration. Easter is a worldwide tradition, an event eclipsed only by Christmas in fame. It's not a military holiday or the birthday of a hero. It's one of the Christian holidays, and it's enjoyed by families everywhere.

Of course, the story of Easter is more than these things. Much more. Easter is a love story, pure and simple . . . and what wondrous love it is.

The work that we do as authors and speakers demands that we do a lot of traveling. And because there are often great distances to go, we usually fly. One of the things we've noticed over the years is that the advertising message of air travel is very simple. The "product" is getting people together, and we've seen this countless times. There's nothing quite as precious as being there. Hugs just aren't the same when they're delivered in cards, letters, or e-mail messages.

What wondrous love is this.

God could have issued a cosmic decree. He could have sent an entourage of angels or a special messenger. But He didn't.

God's love is about showing up. In person. At Christmas we celebrate His coming to earth as a baby. But at Easter we gratefully commemorate His taking the punishment for our sins to appease the anger of a holy God over our shameless and open rebellion. Jesus hung on a cross to redeem us and to say "I love you" with His blood.

From cave-dwellers who scratched symbols of affection to their loved ones on the walls of their stone homes, to amorous lines instantly screaming around the world on the Internet, passionate words have always been a powerful means of one person letting another know that he or she is loved.

Greeting card companies have demonstrated that there are a myriad of ways to successfully communicate these words, but there is only one expression of love that qualifies as "wondrous." A message of love that was written with blood.

When the world shook and the sun was wiped out of heaven,
It was not at the crucifixion, but at the cry from the cross:
The cry which confessed that God was forsaken of God.

—G. K. CHESTERTON

That was the single most significant—and mysterious—moment in the history of all mankind. At the cross a sovereign God who had shown up in person took upon Himself the sins of the world to save the world . . . from Himself.

Why would He do this? There's only one explanation. Because He loved us.

For all have sinned and fall short of the glory of God, and are justified
by his grace, through the redemption that came by Christ Jesus.

—ROMANS 3:23-24

The stories in this book are as remarkable as a blind woman writing thousands of hymns to the glory of the Savior; they're as simple as a melody hummed by

American slaves and as eloquent as the words penned by a wealthy German aristocrat.

But the message of these great hymns is the same. Jesus, all of God in human form, came to stand in the gap between a righteous God and sinful mankind. His death became God's signature scrawled across our emancipation documents. His sacrifice sealed our pardon.

Our prayer is that these stories, and the truths they uncover, will encourage and inspire you. And our hope is that the music will invite you to join us in celebrating the power of this message of God's wondrous love.

Joni Eareckson Tada, Agoura Hills, California

John MacArthur, Sun Valley, California

Robert & Bobbie Wolgemuth, Orlando, Florida

Christ the Lord Is Risen Today

CHARLES WESLEY
1707-1788

"Christ the Lord is ris'n today," Alleluia!
Sons of men and angels say; Alleluia!
Raise your joys and triumphs high; Alleluia!
Sing ye heav'ns, and earth, reply. Alleluia!

Vain the stone, the watch, the seal; Alleluia!
Christ has burst the gates of hell: Alleluia!
Death in vain forbids his rise; Alleluia!
Christ has opened paradise. Alleluia!

Lives again our glorious King; Alleluia!
Where, O death, is now thy sting? Alleluia!
Once he died, our souls to save; Alleluia!
Where thy victory, O grave? Alleluia!

Soar we now where Christ has led, Alleluia!
Foll'wing our exalted Head; Alleluia!
Made like him, like him we rise; Alleluia!
Ours the cross, the grave, the skies, Alleluia!

Hail, the Lord of earth and heav'n! Alleluia!
Praise to thee by both be giv'n; Alleluia!
Thee we greet triumphant now; Alleluia!
Hail, the Resurrection, thou! Alleluia!

AT THE HEART OF THE HYMN
Joni Eareckson Tada

O death, where is thy sting? O grave, where is thy victory?
—1 CORINTHIANS 15:55, KJV

I WISH YOU COULD HAVE BEEN WITH my mother and me on that lovely late spring evening in June 2001. We were on her porch with the ocean to our backs, its breeze in our face, and watched the sun set over the bay. The air was salty, and except for a few gulls crying in the distance, the evening was utterly quiet. The clouds may have been dark and brooding, but the fading sun spread dazzling rays of light across the entire horizon. It was a moment to remember. In fact, it called for a hymn, and so we did what Mom and I always did when watching a lovely sunset. We sang.

Our singing was especially poignant. My mother's health was failing fast, and we knew we wouldn't have her much longer. My husband Ken came out on the back porch to snap a photo of me, Mom, and the sunset. The moment would end up being unforgettable. Two months later, my mother, Lindy Eareckson, went home to be with the Lord Jesus.

My mother's remaining days were filled with suffocating pain and mental anguish. Everything from hallucinations to anxiety attacks, claustrophobia to terrible back pain. It didn't help that she had to wrestle against the blindness of macular degeneration as well as a failing heart and deep fatigue. Old age and mini-strokes were staking their claim on my mother's bright spirit until finally one afternoon while a family friend was reading from my heaven book by her bedside, Mother released a deep sigh and left for Home. I was shocked when I heard the news. On the other hand, I was relieved my mother was now in heaven.

My sisters asked if I would give a short message at our mother's memorial service back in Maryland. At first I balked, thinking that I'd fall apart halfway through; then I realized it would be a chance to honor her among many extended family and friends. I decided yes and asked my husband, Ken, and a few close friends to pray that God would give me an extra measure of grace. He did. My short speech about Mother's life and her love of Christ was indeed a blessing. And I didn't fall apart.

On our flight back to California, I continued to move through the same covering of grace. By the time we arrived at our house, the hour was late, and Ken and I were exhausted. We dropped our suitcases and took a minute to thumb through mail, noticing what were probably a few sympathy cards. I opened the first one addressed from Maryland. Something dropped out of the envelope. When I took a closer look, my chest tightened. It was an obituary from *The Baltimore Sun*. There in print I read: "Margaret J. Eareckson died August 21, 2001." Hot tears filled my eyes. For the first time, I fell apart.

The word *homegoing*, much like *passing away* or *going to be with Jesus*, sounds . . . easier. Easier to swallow than *death* or *died*. But the bare facts in the obituary were as cold and hard as ice.

I shoved the newspaper item aside and bravely opened another card. It was a card of sympathy from my friend Sandy. At least I thought it was a sympathy card. This one, however, looked different. On the front were lilies, and on the inside were the words of "Christ the Lord Is Risen Today." It was an Easter card. Sandy had written, "Joni, somehow this Easter card expresses more what I want to say. Your lively, happy mother is free from pain and isn't it good to know that we will all be reunited at the resurrection. I'm so glad He arose."

Soar we now where Christ has led, Alleluia!
Foll'wing our exalted Head; Alleluia!

Made like him, like him we rise; Alleluia!

Ours the cross, the grave, the skies, Alleluia!

The warmth and joy of the resurrection melted the cold-as-ice fact of my mother's death, releasing the claustrophobic tightness in my chest. Fresh hope and confidence infused me, and in the next moment I almost sang. In fact, I did sing—"Christ the Lord Is Risen Today!" Never were there better words of sympathy than this reminder from my friend of the resurrection of Christ. Because Jesus arose, we have the happy assurance that one day we, too, shall rise and be reunited with our Lord and our loved ones. Oh, joy! My mother is safe and secure, all because Christ our Lord is risen!

Sending an Easter card upon hearing of someone's death? Some might say, "Naah, stick with tradition." I say that tradition can always use an upgrade. And so, in honor of Lindy, I'm holding on to a few Easter cards . . . just in case someone grieving needs a little assurance of the soothing comfort of Christ's resurrection.

IN THE LIGHT OF THE WORD

John MacArthur

NO HYMN MORE PERFECTLY CAPTURES the triumph of Christ's resurrection than this one. It begins with a declaration of the glorious truth discovered by the apostles on resurrection morning: "Christ the Lord is ris'n today."

An angel at the tomb of Christ first made the announcement to Mary Magdalene, Mary the mother of James, and Salome when they went to the tomb to anoint Jesus' body after the Sabbath was over. When they arrived at the tomb, the stone was rolled away, and an angel in a white robe met them inside the burial place. "Don't be alarmed," he said. "You are looking for Jesus the Nazarene, who was crucified. He has risen! He is not here" (Mark 16:6).

After Christ had appeared to Peter, and then to other apostles on the road to Emmaus, the eleven met together in Jerusalem to discuss what had happened. "It is true! The Lord has risen and has appeared to Simon," they said (Luke 24:34). In the familiar words of the King James Version of Scripture, "The Lord is risen indeed."

That proclamation of victory became a common greeting in the early church. "Christ is risen!" someone would say. "He is risen indeed!" was the inevitable reply. The statement and its response are to this day a part of the liturgy in churches worldwide.

The first stanza of this hymn invokes celebration from both heaven and earth ("sons of men and angels"). The hymn-writer calls on the heavens to sing ("Christ is risen!") and earth to reply ("He is risen indeed!"). Alleluia!

"Alleluia" is a Latinized transliteration of the Hebrew *hallelujah*—"Praise God." Every line of every stanza in this hymn is punctuated with the same refrain.

Verse 2 begins with a reference to the extraordinary measures the Romans took to guard the body of Jesus. When Christ's body was removed from the cross, some Pharisees went to Pilate and said, "Sir . . . we remember that while he was still alive that deceiver said, 'After three days I will rise again.' So give the order for the tomb to be made secure until the third day. Otherwise, his disciples may come and steal the body and tell the people that he has been raised from the dead" (Matthew 27:63-64).

"'Take a guard,' Pilate answered. 'Go, make the tomb as secure as you know how.' So they went and made the tomb secure by putting a seal on the stone and posting the guard" (vv. 65-66). But "the stone, the watch, the seal" were all in vain. Christ "burst the gates of hell" (cf. Matthew 16:18); a violent earthquake shook the area; an angel appeared and rolled away the stone; and the Roman guards were so frightened by the appearance of the angel that they "shook and became like dead men" (Matthew 28:4).

"Death in vain forbids his rise." He broke the bonds of death and "was declared with power to be the Son of God by his resurrection from the dead" (Romans 1:4). He thus "opened paradise" to all who believe. Alleluia!

The third stanza borrows language from 1 Corinthians 15, Paul's great discourse on the resurrection. "Where, O death, is your victory? Where, O death, is your sting?" (v. 55). Paul goes on to say, "The sting of death is sin. . . . But thanks be to God! He gives us the victory through our Lord Jesus Christ" (vv. 56-57). In other words, Christ's resurrection signified victory over sin as well as over death.

The final stanza celebrates the fact that we participate in Christ's triumph. The hymn draws once again from Paul's teaching about resurrection in 1 Corinthians 15. Paul wrote, "Just as we have borne the likeness of the earthly man, so shall we bear the likeness of the man from heaven" (v. 49). Elsewhere Paul says that we who believe have spiritual union with Christ in both His death and His resurrection. "If we have been united with him like this in his death, we will certainly also be united with him in his resurrection" (Romans 6:5). We thus participate with Him in "the cross, the grave, the skies." Alleluia!

FROM OUT OF THE PAST
Bobbie Wolgemuth

CHARLES WESLEY WAS THE BRILLIANT AND prolific hymn-writer who led one of the most dramatic and fruitful episodes in church history. He and his brother John were fearless pioneers in the battle for revival and reform in England.

Born the eighteenth child in the family of Susanna and Samuel Wesley, Charles was a friendly boy and cared deeply for others. At home, interaction and sharing were mixed with prayers, Scripture, and the study of Latin. While attending school in London he defended a small Scottish lad against the school bully. Proving his true grit was good preparation for the mobs he would face in his later life.

In college, Charles and John led a group of students called the "Holy Club." This group of friends met to strengthen each other's faith through Bible reading, sharing, singing, and evangelism. Little did they dream that their "methods" of organization would spread revival fire across Europe.

Greatly influenced by devout Moravian Christians, the Wesley brothers ministered to the poor and the outcast. But their energetic evangelistic campaigns and small group meetings were met with fierce opposition. The clergy and society "gentlemen" who wanted to keep the lower classes "in their places" led vicious attacks on the converts and their property.

Meetings led by the Wesleys were held at night in schoolhouses or homes of commoners. Warmed by friendship and a fireplace and candles, the miners, homemakers, unschooled workers, and poor from all over the region would gather for encouragement and teaching. The leader would warmly greet each "parishioner" before teaching a new hymn Charles had written. Line by line, hymns like "O for a Thousand Tongues to Sing" or "Rejoice, the Lord Is King" were repeated, memorized, and heartily sung by the motley crowd.

The subject of the evening would then be introduced by reading another of Wesley's compositions, like "Jesus, Lover of My Soul" or "Love Divine, All Loves Excelling." After instruction, a time of testimony allowed each person to tell "what the Lord had done" since the last meeting. Stories of old habits losing their grip, prayer that was answered in times of distress, strength in weakness, forgiveness of enemies, and deep sorrow over failures were openly shared. The humble folks, with coal grime still on their faces or holding babies in tattered smocks, were lifted out of despondency and spiritual ignorance to knowledge and a great sense of calling.

As the Wesleyan society raised the fallen, set them on their feet, and inspired the socially poor with honesty, industry, and ambition, the opposition grew violent. Rocks were thrown at converts, horses were driven into ponds and drowned, shops were flooded with fire hoses, and homes were vandalized with broken windows and ripped shutters. It was said you could point out where Methodists lived by the condition of their homes. The ruffians were ruthless.

The clergy and gentlemen opposition resented the astonishing success of the movement and the intrusion on their private domain. The converts and leaders were hounded with bulldogs, ducked in deep water, stoned, and threatened with brutality of body, home, and business. Led by the Wesley brothers, the disciples boldly walked amid the scowling faces, singing hymns as they went. They sang their way to eventual victory and the establishment of Methodism.

Summoning spiritual energies equal to the violence, Charles wrote constantly. Using warlike imagery, he issued new hymns daily for use in class meetings. Evangelistic campaigns were fueled with the fire of words set to music. "Soldiers of Christ, Arise" and "Ye Servants of God, Your Master Proclaim" were put in a tract collection entitled "Hymns for Times of Trouble and Persecution."

A fearless soldier of Christ, Charles put to verse the ultimate battle fought with death—apparently lost but finally won. "Christ the Lord Is Risen Today" is the supreme vision for the redeemed society on earth. With exultant voices we sing, "soar we now where Christ has led." The final conquest is victory. "Alleluia!"

What Wondrous Love Is This

AMERICAN FOLK HYMN

What wondrous love is this, O my soul, O my soul,
What wondrous love is this, O my soul!
What wondrous love is this that caused the Lord of bliss
To bear the dreadful curse for my soul, for my soul,
To bear the dreadful curse for my soul!

To God and to the Lamb, I will sing, I will sing,
To God and to the Lamb, I will sing;
To God and to the Lamb, who is the great I AM,
While millions join the theme, I will sing, I will sing,
While millions join the theme, I will sing!

And when from death I'm free, I'll sing on, I'll sing on,
And when from death I'm free, I'll sing on;
And when from death I'm free, I'll sing and joyful be,
And through eternity I'll sing on, I'll sing on,
And through eternity I'll sing on!

At the Heart of the Hymn
Robert Wolgemuth

Greater love has no one than this, that someone lays down his life for his friends.
—John 15:13, esv

Most of my friends played Little League baseball. Looking back, I actually don't remember asking my dad if I could get involved. Maybe I already knew that he would have suggested that it was more important to keep up with my homework or help around the house. Regardless, I didn't ask, and so I didn't participate in Little League . . . until almost fifty years later.

In August 2000, soon after we moved to Florida, our twelve-year-old godson was getting ready to sign up for fall Little League. His dad, Orel Hershiser, had recently retired from a seventeen-year Major League career and was going to be the manager of the team.

"Why don't you sign up to be one of my coaches?" Orel asked me one morning over the phone.

Saying "no thanks" to the offer didn't cross my mind.

Not having any experience on the playing or coaching side of Little League, I volunteered to be the team's official "go-for." My tasks included carrying equipment, helping the boys straighten up the dugout (the other coaches dubbed me "Coach Manners"), and learning how to rake the infield and line the field. I also did some of the bench coaching. It was my job to post the names of the boys who were going to play each inning on the little magnetic roster we hung with a wire on the wall of the dugout.

One of the rules of Little League is that every boy must play at least one inning in every game, even the kids who are "still working on their skills." Yes, even the youngster who, in twelve games, not only struck out every time, but never once made contact with the ball.

Informing a boy that I was taking him out of the game for another player soon became the least favorite part of my job. Seeing an eager competitor looking for his name on the board and not finding it was a study in hopelessness.

"Coach Wolgemuth," he'd plead. "I want to play. Let me stay in the game. Please."

Maybe this was hard for me because I understand my own strong desire to keep doing the things I love to do—and to avoid the things I don't enjoy . . . like sitting on the bench.

But what if the assignment is something difficult, or dangerous, or life-threatening? What if our appeal is, "Please *don't* make me go there. I'd *rather* stay here on the bench"?

Of the hundreds of stories that have come out of the attack on the World Trade Center on September 11, 2001, perhaps the most incredible have been told about courageous paramedics, firefighters, and police officers. While thousands were running *from* the crumbling buildings to save their own lives, these heroes were running *into* the buildings to save others.

As a result, hundreds of these men and women—selfless American heroes—were crushed and lost when the buildings collapsed.

Just a few hours before His trial and crucifixion, Jesus gathered His disciples together. He told them that His hour had come. "You are My friends," he told them. "My life is about to be sacrificed for you."

They must have been stunned by the news. This was an assignment none of them would have willingly volunteered for.

But what these men didn't understand was what Jesus meant by "friends."

Certainly Jesus was including the twelve who had left their families and their careers to follow Him. Undependable and thickheaded as they were, they loved

Jesus. They had seen, heard, and felt wonderful things that had drawn them to the Master. They *were* His friends.

But like the brave men and women on September 11 rushing into the flaming skyscrapers, Jesus also considered complete strangers as His friends.

For God so loved the world, that he gave his only son.
—JOHN 3:16, ESV

That day on the cross, Jesus died for people who had never known Him, met Him, or even seen Him. These people—the apostle John called them "the world"—were His friends, and He was willing to bleed and die for them too.

But the most indescribable fact of Jesus' death on the cross was that He also considered His foes to be His friends. These were men and women who despised Him—even those perpetrators who plotted His execution.

Friend, do what you came to do.
—JESUS TO JUDAS IN THE GARDEN; MATTHEW 26:50, ESV

Father, forgive them, for they know not what they do.
—JESUS FROM THE CROSS; LUKE 23:34, ESV

Like the youngsters on the bench, you and I long to be given the assignments we enjoy. Relationships with those we enjoy. Work that satisfies us. Responsibilities that give us pleasure. "Put me in, Coach. Put me in."

But Jesus not only went to the cross for those who loved Him and those who didn't know Him, but He gave Himself for those who loathed Him. He embraced friends, strangers, and adversaries. His love included them all.

What wondrous love is this!

IN THE LIGHT OF THE WORD
John MacArthur

*T*HIS SPLENDID AMERICAN FOLK HYMN celebrates the truth of John 15:13: "Greater love has no one than this, that one lay down his life for his friends." Christ's love for sinners is made even more wondrous when we realize that He is "the Lord of bliss." He gave up ruling over all heaven's delights to come to earth and humble Himself on a cross.

Philippians 2:5-8 describes what Christ gave up in order to die: "Being in very nature God, [He] did not consider equality with God something to be grasped, but made himself nothing, taking the very nature of a servant, being made in human likeness. And being found in appearance as a man, he humbled himself and became obedient to death—even death on a cross!" He went from the most exalted position in heaven to the most debased and degrading position on earth.

And why did He do this? "To bear the dreadful curse for my soul." That refers to the curse of sin. When Adam sinned, he brought a curse and divine condemnation on all humanity. Romans 5:18 says, "The result of one trespass was condemnation for all men."

But we are not guilty merely because of what Adam did. We have also each sinned individually and repeatedly (Romans 3:23), contributing to the effects of the curse. Isaiah 24:5-6 says, "The earth is defiled by its people; they have disobeyed the laws, violated the statutes and broken the everlasting covenant. Therefore a curse consumes the earth; its people must bear their guilt."

The thought of bearing our own guilt ought to terrify us. Each of us could say with the psalmist, "My guilt has overwhelmed me like a burden too heavy to bear" (Psalm 38:4). Those are the simple facts of sin and condemnation.

But the wonderful truth of the Gospel is that Christ has borne the guilt of His people so that they don't have to bear it anymore. "He himself bore our sins in his body on the tree" (1 Peter 2:24). In the words of our hymn, He "[bore] the dreadful curse for my soul." He took upon Himself both the guilt and the punishment for our sins.

Someone had to pay the debt of sin. Someone had to suffer the dreadful curse. It was far too much for any sinner to bear. We could spend an eternity in hell and still not have begun to pay the price of our own sin. So Jesus paid that price for us in full.

And conversely, the full merit of Jesus' righteousness is imputed to us. Scripture says, "God made him who had no sin to be sin for us, so that in him we might become the righteousness of God" (2 Corinthians 5:21). In other words, on the cross God treated Jesus as if He had lived my life, so that God could treat me as if I had lived Christ's life. Our transgressions are paid for; our sin is covered, and Christ's own righteousness is freely imputed to our account (Romans 4:4-8).

So the cross was a vicarious punishment for sin, and Christ, dying there, was like a sacrificial Lamb "who takes away the sin of the world!" (John 1:29).

Stanza 2 is a paean of thankfulness "To God and to the Lamb" for the glorious work of our salvation. When the hymn-writer identifies the Lamb as "the great I AM," he is acknowledging the deity of Christ, employing the covenant name of Jehovah from Exodus 3:14. This is a profound expression of worship, and as stanza 3 suggests, it is the very kind of worship we'll sing "through eternity."

Hebrews 9:28 says, "Christ was sacrificed once to take away the sins of many people; and he will appear a second time, not to bear sin, but to bring salvation to those who are waiting for him." We look forward eagerly to that day, and the eternity to follow, where "millions [will] join the theme" of praise to the Lamb, whose wondrous love for us exceeds every other kind of love known on earth.

From Out of the Past

Bobbie Wolgemuth

ONE OF THE BEST KNOWN OF OUR AMERICAN FOLK HYMNS is "What Wondrous Love Is This." It was probably composed by American mountain people and handed down orally and preserved for our hymnbooks. The text of the hymn demonstrates the passion of faith coming from a community of people brimming with ripe fruits of the Spirit.

Enjoying a simpler pace of life, solitude, and serenity, these plain folks maintained the memory and meaning of their faith by singing. They knew well the art of connecting with one another, whether hunting on the ridge, quilting together with neighbors, or shelling lima beans on the porch with their families. It was in these times and places that the blueprint of their spiritual heritage was passed on in musical form.

The melody for the hymn is simple and haunting. Phrases are repeated over and over, like a mother's words to her children when she wants to make sure they get the point. With simplicity, the musical quality takes us down to the sinking places with minor-sounding tones and then lifts us up with the hope of eternity through the words. Like pieces of scraps sewn together to tell a story, this hymn is a beautiful patchwork of folk art.

It was a South Carolina musician, William Walker, who first put "What Wondrous Love Is This" into a collection entitled "The Southern Harmony and Musical Companion" in 1835. William would compile melodies he discovered from travels around southern Appalachia and camp meetings.

With no seminary training, these simple mountain people have given us a powerful faith lesson in an unforgettable form. God has indeed chosen the poor of this world to be rich in faith.

Their voices, never to be silenced, will sing on.

Were You There?

SPIRITUAL

Were you there when they crucified my Lord?
Were you there when they crucified my Lord?
Oh! Sometimes it causes me to tremble, tremble, tremble.
Were you there when they crucified my Lord?

Were you there when they nailed him to the tree?
Were you there when they nailed him to the tree?
Oh! Sometimes it causes me to tremble, tremble, tremble.
Were you there when they nailed him to the tree?

Were you there when they pierced him in the side?
Were you there when they pierced him in the side?
Oh! Sometimes it causes me to tremble, tremble, tremble.
Were you there when they pierced him in the side?

Were you there when they laid him in the tomb?
Were you there when they laid him in the tomb?
Oh! Sometimes it causes me to tremble, tremble, tremble.
Were you there when they laid him in the tomb?

Were you there when he rose up from the dead?
Were you there when he rose up from the dead?
Oh! Sometimes I feel like shouting glory, glory, glory!
Were you there when he rose up from the dead?

At the Heart of the Hymn
Robert Wolgemuth

I am crucified with Christ, nevertheless I live.
—Galatians 2:20, kjv

Don't you just hate to miss things?

A few years ago I walked into my office. A couple of my friends were engaged in animated conversation. "What's up?" I asked.

"The concert last night down at the Performing Arts Center was incredible . . . were you there?"

"No, I didn't hear anything about it," I responded, completely frustrated at missing one of my favorite groups in concert.

Of course, my friends went on to explain in intricate detail what went on the night before. If only I had known . . . but I didn't. I would have loved to witness this special concert, but I missed it. I spent the rest of the morning with a knot in my stomach, angry that no one had told me about the evening and regretting that I hadn't been paying attention enough to know about it. I'll never get another chance.

Do you know how this feels? Do you hate to miss things too?

When I'm at a Major League baseball game, I always wait until between innings to grab a hot dog or something to drink. Sometimes I literally run to and from the concession areas under the grandstands. Sure, they have television monitors in these areas, but that doesn't make any difference. I'd be so upset if I missed seeing a spectacular catch or a line drive home run with my own eyes. Instant replays just aren't the same.

For you and me, whether celebrations or crises, many of the most important moments and events that have shaped history happened before we were born . . . or when we were too young to remember . . . or when we were somewhere else.

In the twentieth century alone, there were many of these. Archduke Franz Ferdinand of Austria-Hungary being assassinated by Serbian activists, starting World War I; twenty thousand American soldiers landing on the beaches of Normandy like a giant wave crashing onto the sand; a pristine Sunday morning on the island of Oahu with hundreds of Japanese Zeroes pummeling the naval base at Pearl Harbor; the grassy knoll in downtown Dallas and a sniper's bullet finding our thirty-fifth president; nineteen terrorists commandeering four commercial airplanes, maneuvering three of them into huge buildings like guided missiles.

You and I probably missed these epic events; we weren't there. Sure, we've seen or heard replays of them, but it's not the same as if we'd actually been there ourselves. And whether we were on location or not, these events changed the world and shaped our lives.

Two millennia ago, on a hill just outside the city of Jerusalem, something incredible happened. Jesus Christ, the sinless Son of a holy God, died like a common criminal. This event, like none other, changed the course of human history. Nothing before and nothing since has had such a profound effect on the world's inhabitants—past, present, or future. And none of us were there to see it.

But there *were* eyewitnesses . . . and it's not who you think.

In nineteenth-century America, men and women were brought to America on slave ships, most of them from the African continent. Once purchased by land owners, they had no rights, no possessions, and no freedom.

They had no means of transportation, but they *could* travel. Through time and space, like science fiction heroes, they went to Calvary.

Were you there when they crucified my Lord?

"Of course not," one of them might have said. "This happened more than eighteen hundred years ago."

Were you there when they nailed him to the tree?

"Don't be ridiculous."

Were you there when they laid him in the tomb?

Thirty questions and the answer to each one is an unequivocal "no." The most important event of all time—and they missed it. No, they *weren't* there.

Or were they?

Slaves were literally torn from their parents' arms, packed into ships like common cartage, and transported across an ocean. On the auction block they endured untold humiliation. Can you imagine it? These people introduced the world to a kind of suffering few had ever known—the scourge of undeserved punishment and the betrayal of all humanity.

But in their pain and isolation, they were dramatically transported back to the first century. Their hearts became inextricably bound to the Savior with whom they identified so completely.

And through their suffering these men and women became spiritual eyewitnesses to the cross, the nails, and the tomb. As they swung their axes to soften the stubborn soil, they heard the sound of the soldiers driving nails into the Savior's hands and feet. Yes, they *were* there. When their taskmasters beat them for sport, they felt the sword plunging into His side. Yes, they *were* there.

And although their circumstances shouted meaninglessness and loss, their hearts swelled at the promise of resurrection. *Were you there when he rose up from the dead?*

This alone brought them hope. Jesus had liberated their souls.

Whether our trials are part of our past, our present, or inevitably waiting for us tomorrow, we have the chance to personally visit the cross and the tomb. We can invite the Savior into our experiences and be miraculously transported to this historic scene.

And we can join those who saw His resurrected body . . . and touched Him. Our wounded hearts can be filled with the blessed hope of seeing it for ourselves, just like Mary, John, the Roman guards, and these beloved slaves.

We can go there. We can go there right now. We don't have to miss it.

Sometimes it causes me to tremble.

IN THE LIGHT OF THE WORD
John MacArthur

THIS CLASSIC SPIRITUAL BUILDS TO A powerful crescendo by highlighting a different detail of the crucifixion in each stanza, culminating with a triumphant celebration of the resurrection. Meanwhile, it evokes a poignantly personal perspective on the drama of the cross by asking the question, "Were you there. . . ?"—compelling us to contemplate the cross from the viewpoint of an eyewitness.

The first stanza introduces the *fact* of the crucifixion: "Were you there when they crucified my Lord?" Crucifixion was a cruel punishment designed to prolong the pain and terror of death. Victims were sometimes kept alive in agony for days. It was a form of execution reserved for the lowest type of criminal— and never for Roman citizens. Crucifixion was always a horrible spectacle, but in this case wicked men were unjustly killing "my Lord"—"the Lord of glory" (1 Corinthians 2:8).

The refrain is therefore fitting: "Sometimes it causes me to tremble." It was both an incongruity and an immense injustice that Christ, who was "holy, blameless, pure, set apart from sinners, [and] exalted above the heavens" (Hebrews 7:26), would die in such an ignominious manner between two thieves. It *ought* to cause us to tremble when we think of it.

The second stanza asks, "Were you there when they nailed him to the tree?" The nails used in Roman crucifixions were large, tapered iron spikes, similar to railroad spikes, but slightly longer and much thinner. The person being crucified would be forced to lie down on the cross with arms extended, while the nails were driven through the flesh and into the wood of the cross with seven to ten heavy blows from a large hammer. The nails were placed not through the palms of the hands as is often thought, but through the wrists. (The tendons and bone structure of human hands are insufficiently strong to support the body's entire weight.) The nails shattered bones and damaged nerves as they passed though the wrists, causing unbearably intense pain in both arms. That is why victims were offered myrrh (a mild narcotic) just before the nails were driven through (Mark 15:23). This was not for mercy's sake, but to keep the victim from lapsing into unconsciousness because of the severity of the pain.

Usually then a single nail was driven through both feet, between the ankle bones and the Achilles tendon. The extreme agony of such wounds was only intensified when the cross was stood up and dropped into a hole. And there the cross would stand erect while hours passed slowly and the victim writhed in indescribable agony.

The fourth stanza asks, "Were you there when they laid him in the tomb?" John 19:38-41 says Joseph of Arimathea and Nicodemus, both influential men in Jerusalem, asked Pilate for the body of Christ, bought embalming spices and linen, and hastily wrapped the body and laid it in a new tomb in a garden.

No one seemed to expect Him to rise from the dead, even though He had repeatedly told them He would. But "early on the first day of the week" (John 20:1) He broke the bonds of death, emerged from His tomb, and began a series of appearances to His disciples—appearing to as many as five hundred of them on one occasion (1 Corinthians 15:5-6). As the fourth stanza of the spiritual says, "Sometimes I feel like shouting glory, glory, glory!"

FROM OUT OF THE PAST

Bobbie Wolgemuth

EVERY CULTURE IS DEFINED BY A UNIQUE LANGUAGE. And this language binds the people together, creating a safe place that surrounds and protects them from others.

For tens of thousands of illiterate slaves brought to America during the eighteenth century, singing became their language—their unique and unbreakable means of communication.

It's hard to imagine the conditions these people had to suffer. Longing for a sense of worth and self-respect, men, women, and children were bought and sold like farm animals by their owners. Slaves worked the fields like oxen and were sometimes beaten for sport.

In America, slaves—mostly Africans—encountered Christianity for the first time. But it's understandable that many slaves fought against a religion that was hypocritical, a religion practiced by many slaveholders who publicly promoted the ideals of love and mercy, yet regularly mistreated them.

Still, these spiritual people were fascinated with Bible characters. Many of the biblical heroes faced impossible situations like their own: David confronting

Goliath with only a sling, Joshua's army marching around the ominous walls of Jericho with just trumpets, and Jesus defying His captors by conquering death.

As slaves, no freedoms or personal rights were theirs . . . except for two. Once a week they were permitted to meet for Christian services, and they were allowed to sing.

Farmhands and their families would gather outside church buildings or plantation "praise houses" to hear itinerant ministers recount these wonderful biblical narratives. Even though slaves were not allowed inside, they still experienced the power of the music. And following the meeting the slaves continued singing, sometimes for hours. Most slave owners allowed "quiet songs" but no dancing or drums. Regardless of these restrictions, music filled the hearts of the slaves with hope.

Because they needed to share their joys and sorrows, pains and hopes, courageous slaves also held clandestine "camp meetings" or "bush meetings" at secret places. Once-a-week church services weren't enough. They sang—and sometimes danced to—the precursors of spirituals, which they called "corn ditties." And between meetings slaves were sometimes allowed to softly sing in the fields.

In time these "ditties" became "spirituals." Uplifting verses, covert cultural expressions of social commentary, and a code language of resistance and defiance soon became the deepest expression of the slave's only hope in the saving grace of Jesus Christ. Clever tunes were transformed into musical expressions of transcendence and peace.

"Were You There?" has no known lyricist or composer. There is no record of when it was first sung. However, we know that this spiritual—and many others like it—became the language of a people who knew Jesus. People who were not capable of moving freely from place to place, but people who by these hymns successfully transported their souls to the cross, to the tomb, and to glory.

He Was Wounded for Our Transgressions

THOMAS CHISHOLM
1866-1960

He was wounded for our transgressions,
He bore our sins in his body on the tree;
For our guilt he gave us peace, from our bondage gave release,
And with his stripes, and with his stripes,
And with his stripes our souls are healed.

He was numbered among transgressors,
We did esteem him forsaken by his God;
As our sacrifice he died, that the law be satisfied,
And all our sin, and all our sin,
And all our sin was laid on him.

We had wandered, we all had wandered
Far from the fold of "the Shepherd of the sheep";
But he sought us where we were, on the mountains bleak and bare,
And brought us home, and brought us home,
And brought us safely home to God.

Who can number his generation?
Who shall declare all the triumphs of his cross?
Millions dead now live again, myriads follow in his train!
Victorious Lord, victorious Lord,
Victorious Lord and coming King!

AT THE HEART OF THE HYMN

Robert Wolgemuth

Love your enemies and pray for those who persecute you, that you may be sons of your Father in heaven.

—MATTHEW 5:44

DO YOU HAVE ANY ENEMIES?

Michael Butler was a self-described industrialist, millionaire, sportsman, and playboy. He liked polo, parties, and pop art. During the sixties he was a friend and adviser to John Kennedy, got high with Mick Jagger, and horsed around with Prince Charles.[1]

A generous contributor to the Democratic Party, Michael Butler was introduced to the widest swath of the American public in 1973 when he showed up in a report issued by the Joint Committee on Internal Revenue Taxation. Michael Butler was one of a handful of people on President Richard Nixon's notorious "Enemies List." According to accounts, the President ordered the IRS to pursue and harass certain individuals whom he saw as adversaries, threats to his political power base. Richard Nixon considered the flamboyant Michael Butler his enemy.

Not surprisingly, the feelings were mutual. Michael Butler was vocal in his contempt for Richard Nixon.

You and I may not go so far as to actually publish a list of people we don't like, but most of us have one.

When I was a little boy growing up in Waynesboro, Pennsylvania, Van Arrow was our neighborhood bully. He had dark hair and eyes as black as night. And he was very big—at least to us. For no reason, Van Arrow would break up our games and chase us back to our homes. My brothers and I trembled at the sound of his name.

Van Arrow would be on my list.

Because I was a late bloomer, often the smallest boy in school, there were other Van Arrows in my life. Young men often look for ways to inflate their own egos by lording it over little kids like me. They, too, would have made my list.

During my adolescence, I got along with most everyone . . . although there *were* a few kids at school whose names would show up on my inventory of least favorite. As a grownup, although I'd rather not admit it, I guess that I have an informal list of folks I don't like. People whose predispositions about me never gave me a chance. People who treated me unfairly in business.

And before you get too judgmental, you probably have an unwritten list too.

One of the sobering realities of this story is that you and I may be on someone else's list. In fact, I know for certain that we used to be on a very serious enemies list.

If, when we were God's enemies, we were reconciled to him through the death of his Son, how much more, having been reconciled, shall we be saved through his life!
—ROMANS 5:10

Jesus Christ stood between the wrath of a holy God and the eternal condemnation of sinful mankind—that's you and me. And through His death, He literally saved our lives. What that means is that we were on God's enemies list, but through the blood of His Son, our names have been removed. Jesus did that by putting His name where ours had been and dying like a common criminal.

He was numbered among transgressors,
We did esteem him forsaken by his God;

As our sacrifice he died, that the law be satisfied,

And all our sin was laid on him.

And now that God has removed us from His doomed list, our charge is to love people—even those who deserve to be on our enemies list—just as He loved us.

> *This is how everyone will recognize that you are my disciples, when they see the love you have for each other.*
>
> —JOHN 13:35 (THE MESSAGE)

1. Rick Kogan, "The Aging of Aquarius," *Chicago Tribune Magazine,* June 1996.

IN THE LIGHT OF THE WORD
John MacArthur

THE FAMILIAR WORDS OF ISAIAH 53 have been poetically adapted for this hymn, which describes the sufferings of Christ on the cross through the eyes of a prophet who lived more than seven hundred years before Christ.

Isaiah 53 is one of my favorite passages of Scripture. Like Psalm 22, it describes the crucifixion of Christ with pinpoint accuracy in every detail, giving graphic and powerful proof that the Bible was inspired by God. The work of mere men could never foretell future events with such perfect precision and rich theological insight.

Isaiah 53 is a profound exposition of the *theological meaning* of Christ's atoning work. According to Isaiah, the sacrifice of the Suffering Servant was a vicarious atonement (v. 10). Christ's anguish and death on the cross was a punishment for sins of which He was not guilty—but we are. He suffered in our place. "He took up our infirmities and carried our sorrows" (v. 4). "He was pierced for our transgressions, he was crushed for our iniquities" (v. 5). "The LORD has laid on him the iniquity of us all" (v. 6). "For the transgression of my people he was stricken" (v. 8). He died as a substitute for others; His suffering was the price of atonement for their sin.

The hymn-writer borrows the second line of his first stanza from a New Testament source—1 Peter 2:24, where Peter writes: "He himself bore our sins in his body on the tree, so that we might die to sins and live for righteousness; by his wounds you have been healed." Notice that the apostle Peter was also quoting from Isaiah 53:5: "By his wounds we are healed." The hymn-writer adapts that phrase for the closing line of his first stanza.

Stanza 2 continues with words borrowed from Isaiah 53:12: "He . . . was numbered with the transgressors"—a reference to the fact that Christ was crucified as a common criminal. He was treated with the contempt due the lowest sinner, even though He was perfectly sinless. Line 2 of the second stanza echoes Isaiah 53:4: "We considered him stricken by God, smitten by him, and afflicted."

Indeed, to a bystander at the cross it would have appeared that the full force of God's wrath against sin was being poured out on His own Son! And the amazing truth is, that is *precisely* what was happening. Isaiah writes: "It was the LORD's will to crush him and cause him to suffer . . . [to make] his life a guilt offering" (v. 10). Christ was, in a spiritual sense, forsaken by God on the cross (cf. Matt. 27:46). God was punishing His own sinless Son for others' sins!

The second stanza of our hymn closes with a reference to the end of verse 6: "The LORD has laid on him the iniquity of us all." Then the third stanza refers back to the first part of that same verse. It portrays sinners as lost and wandering sheep, brought safely home by the loving Great Shepherd. This imagery of sheep and Shepherd is a common theme in Scripture (Psalm 23; 79:13; 80:1; Isaiah 40:11; Jeremiah 23:3-4; Ezekiel 34:11-12, 23; John 10:11, 14, 27-30; Hebrews 13:20; 1 Peter 2:25).

The closing stanza of the hymn is a celebration of the triumph of the cross. The opening line of that stanza is drawn from Isaiah 53:8: "And who can speak of his descendants?" The hymn-writer interprets that phrase as a statement about the vast numbers who are redeemed because the Suffering Servant bore their sins. Isaiah also highlights that same truth in the biblical text: "By his knowledge my righteous servant will justify *many,* and he will bear their iniquities" (v. 11). "He bore the sin of *many"* (v. 12).

There seems to be a parallel in the biblical text between verse 8 ("who can speak of his descendants?") and verse 10 ("The LORD . . . will see his offspring"). Bystanders at the cross were unable to see this glorious reality from God's perspective. To them, it looked like a stunning defeat for Christ. His life was snuffed out horribly. He appeared to be utterly defeated, having been abandoned by His own disciples, childless, friendless, and literally God-forsaken.

But God viewed the cross as the greatest victory of all time. As the hymn-writer so beautifully states, the triumphs of the cross are innumerable. Multitudes once spiritually dead are now alive in Christ. In eternity they will be like the stars of heaven and the sands of the seashore—vast and measureless.

FROM OUT OF THE PAST

Bobbie Wolgemuth

*L*ACK OF FORMAL EDUCATION AND FRAIL HEALTH did not stop Thomas Obadiah Chisholm from writing some of the most moving hymns in American history. As a boy, Thomas attended a little country school in his hometown of Franklin, Kentucky. His family lived in a rustic log cabin where he learned that neither money nor education came easily. Without the benefit of a high school degree or any formal training, he began to teach other children at the one-room schoolhouse when he was just sixteen years old. The industrious self-taught lad loved writing and became the associate editor of his hometown weekly paper, *The Franklin Favorite,* when he was twenty-one.

Life dramatically changed when he attended a revival meeting conducted by Dr. Henry Clay Morrison, founder of Asbury College and Theological Seminary in Wilmore, Kentucky. Affirming the presence and the potential of spiritual passion displayed by young Thomas, Dr. Morrison himself mentored the new convert.

For the next ten years Thomas became a student of the Bible and was ordained to the Methodist ministry as a traveling preacher when he was thirty-seven. For a short time he pastored a church in Scottsville, Kentucky, but the demands of ministry were too strenuous for his weak health. Leaving the preaching ministry, he turned his evangelistic efforts to pen and paper. Forced to make ends meet because his writing provided little income, he sold insurance. Continuing to write spiritual poems, he sent them to various magazines and publishers, hoping for an occasional acceptance letter.

One of the poems that expressed Thomas's gratitude to God received a hearty acceptance letter from an editor at Hope Publishing Company. "Great Is Thy Faithfulness" was set to music and found its way into ministry worldwide through the Billy Graham crusades. His desire that every one of his works have a message for human hearts true to the Word of God was fulfilled in the over twelve hundred hymns he wrote.

Chisholm had a long and fruitful ministry notwithstanding the disappointments of health and career. He wrote favorite and familiar hymn texts for "O to Be Like Thee!" and "Living for Jesus." When Chisholm was seventy-five years old he wrote "He Was Wounded for Our Transgressions." A lifetime of experiencing God's faithfulness produced the confident declaration of the triumphs of the cross. "Victorious Lord and coming King!"

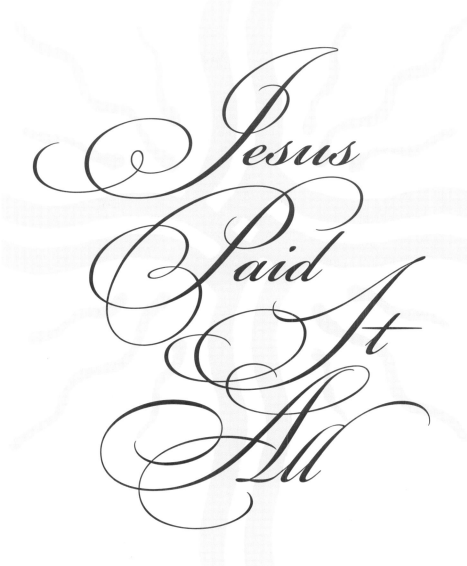

ELVINA M. HALL
1820-1869

JOHN T. GRAPE
1835-1915

I hear the Savior say, "Your strength indeed is small,
Child of weakness, watch and pray,
Find in me your all in all."

Chorus:
Jesus paid it all, all to him I owe;
Sin had left a crimson stain, he washed it white as snow.

Lord, now indeed I find your power, and yours alone,
Can change the leper's spots,
And melt the heart of stone.

For nothing good have I whereby your grace to claim—
I'll wash my garments white
In the blood of Calv'ry's Lamb.

And when, before the throne, I stand in him complete,
"Jesus died my soul to save,"
My lips shall still repeat.

AT THE HEART OF THE HYMN
Joni Eareckson Tada

Ye are not your own . . . ye are bought with a price: therefore glorify God in your body, and in your spirit, which are God's.

—1 CORINTHIANS 6:19-20, KJV

MY HUSBAND DOESN'T KEEP TABS ON ME, doesn't keep a scorecard, and we don't do the tit-for-tat thing, but Ken *will* say to me when there's good reason, "You owe me one."

In the early years of our marriage, those words along with the look in his eye used to give me the jitters. As if I *really* did owe him; not for just one obligation, but many. As anniversaries came and went, I noticed that he never tried to collect. Soon I caught on. This whole "you owe me one" thing is for fun. It's just one of those cute jabs. It's lighthearted because we both understand there is no way either of us can or should pay back what's owed. That's not the nature of love.

It's not the nature of God's love either. Sometimes we forget that. I've often heard people say, "Jesus died for me, and I owe Him such a great debt. It's so great, in fact, that I'll never be able to pay Him back."

But wait a minute. It's *not* a matter of owing God anything. There is no debt for you to pay. Romans 6:23 says, "The wages of sin is death, but the gift of God is eternal life in Christ Jesus our Lord." Isn't that wonderful? Salvation is a gift. And when a gift is given, there is no debt, nothing for you to pay back. If you even entertained the thought, it could almost be insulting.

How so? My wedding anniversary is coming up, and Ken may very well give me a wonderful gift. I would not dream of opening up his present—let's say it's something super-expensive—I wouldn't think of unwrapping it and saying, "Oh, dear

Ken, I'm overwhelmed . . . oh, my, I really owe you one. How am I ever going to pay you back?" I wouldn't do that because it would lessen the gift. It would make it "not a gift," tainting his expression of love.

It's the same way with the gift of salvation. When Christ went to the cross for you, He did so, not expecting you to pay Him back. Don't even think about it.

Lebanon is not sufficient for altar fires, nor its animals enough for burnt offerings.

—ISAIAH 40:16

In other words, there aren't enough cedars in Lebanon to kindle an altar fire for all the cattle that it would take to even begin to make an adequate offering. It's not a matter of duty or debt or what is owed or what should be paid back.

It is a gift. And what do you do with gifts? You receive them and say thank you. And then you live in such a way as to honor and please the one who has given so much. It's as 1 John 4:19 says: "We love [Him] because he first loved us." Our obedience and service is simply an effervescent, happy-hearted response of sheer love for who He is and what He has given.

Which brings me to the first line in the refrain of this wonderful hymn.

Jesus paid it all, all to him I owe;
Sin had left a crimson stain, he washed it white as snow.

Hymn-writer John T. Grape was without doubt enthralled at the incalculable price that Jesus paid when He redeemed sinful man on the cross. So infinitely precious was His death that he wrote, "All to him I owe." At the risk of putting words in Mr. Grape's mouth, I think I know what he was saying . . .

Jesus paid it all, and there is nothing—absolutely nothing—you can add. All you can do is live your life as one big *thank you.*

IN THE LIGHT OF THE WORD

John MacArthur

PROVERBS 24:10 SAYS, "If you falter in times of trouble, how small is your strength!" Who has not faltered in times of trouble? Our strength "indeed *is* small," and this familiar hymn pays tribute to that fact while pointing us to Christ as our "all in all"—our whole strength and sustenance not only in times of trouble, but "in all" of life's experiences.

Each stanza of the hymn contains the same two themes: the sinner's utter weakness, and Christ's infinite power to cleanse us from sin. The refrain is a succinct statement of the doctrine of justification: "Jesus paid it all, all to him I owe; sin had left a crimson stain, he washed it white as snow." The refrain is based on Isaiah 1:18: "'Come now, let us reason together,' says the LORD. 'Though your sins are like scarlet, they shall be as white as snow; though they are red as crimson, they shall be like wool.'"

Every genuine believer must give testimony to the truth of this hymn's signature line. "Jesus paid it all, all to him I owe." Nothing we could ever do would atone for our own sin. Our own works contribute nothing toward our salvation. Christ paid the debt in full, and there is nothing for us to add. "He saved us, not because of righteous things we had done, but because of his mercy. He saved us through the washing of rebirth and renewal by the Holy Spirit" (Titus 3:5).

Stanza 2 makes reference to the believer's rebirth by the Spirit of God. Only the Lord's power—and that alone—can change sinful hearts and cleanse the effects of sin. That is exactly what Titus 3:5 says occurs at regeneration: "washing . . . and renewal by the Holy Spirit."

The hymn-writer speaks of "chang[ing] the leper's spots" and "melt[ing] the heart of stone." Leprosy caused ceremonial defilement according to Moses' Law (Leviticus 13:42-46) and is therefore a fitting illustration of sin. Sin may be thought of as a spiritual leprosy, because it is infectious and results in nothing but defilement and decay. Jesus demonstrated His power over leprosy by healing it instantly and completely (Mark 1:40-42). That symbolized His power over every kind of uncleanness, including the spiritual defilement of sin.

The reference to a "heart of stone" harks back to Ezekiel 36:26, where the salvation of Israel is prophetically described: "I will give you a new heart and put a new spirit in you; I will remove from you your heart of stone and give you a heart of flesh." That is the same work Christ does in each believer at the moment of regeneration.

Stanza 3 opens with another confession of the believer's spiritual bankruptcy: "Nothing good have I whereby your grace to claim." Even the apostle Paul wrote, "nothing good lives in me, that is, in my sinful nature" (Romans 7:18). Grace is by definition utterly undeserved, unmerited, and unattainable by those who try to work for it (see Romans 4:4-5). Our only hope for redemption from our sin is to trust in the grace of God.

Stanza 3 also contains a reference to Revelation 7:13-14, where the apostle John saw a vision of some martyrs in heaven. He writes, "Then one of the elders asked me, 'These in white robes—who are they, and where did they come from?' I answered, 'Sir, you know.' And he said, 'These are they who have come out of the great tribulation; they have washed their robes and made them white in the blood of the Lamb.'"

Stanza 4 looks forward to heaven. The worshiper confesses that even in the glorious perfection of heaven, when we finally "stand in him complete," remade in His perfect likeness (1 John 3:2), we will confess (and "still repeat") that we owe everything to *His* saving work alone.

FROM OUT OF THE PAST
Bobbie Wolgemuth

*I*T WAS AN ORDINARY WOMAN PARISHIONER who was bestowed with the gift of poetry that became this much-loved Communion hymn. It happened halfway through the morning service at the Monument Street Methodist Church in Baltimore, Maryland. Mrs. Elvina Hall sang in the choir and had been a faithful church member since her childhood. This Sunday would be forever marked in her life as the day an unusual gift was given to her.

The forty-five-year-old woman heard a voice so strong she rummaged through her purse during the sermon to find paper to write down the words being formed in her mind. Not finding anything but a pencil, she opened to the flyleaf of her hymnal and began scribbling the words. As if taking shorthand for the thoughts being dictated to her, she wrote, "I hear the Savior say, 'Your strength indeed is small, child of weakness watch and pray, find in me your all in all.'"

Before the minister, Reverend George Schrick, finished his message, Mrs. Hall had written the verses, but no refrain had been given to her. That was given to a coal merchant, John Grape, who was also the organist and director of the Monument Street church choir. He was not a professional musician but liked to compose tunes in his free time. While at home one day, he had written a tune that only his wife so far had admired. He entitled the chorus "All to Christ I Owe" and handed a copy to the minister.

Mrs. Hall eventually gave the words of her poem to Reverend Schrick, probably telling him that the subject of his sermon had so moved her that the stanzas written on the inside of the hymnbook cover were the inspired result. It was this gracious pastor who remembered the tune title composed by the organist and encouraged the blending of the two.

The tune was a perfect marriage with the four verses composed by Elvina Hall. Mr. Grape's refrain was now admired by all in the church, not just his wife alone.

Three years later the hymn first appeared in a hymnal, just one year before Mrs. Hall's early death at age forty-nine. No doubt at her funeral the story was told of two ordinary church workers who were inspirationally given pieces of a musical puzzle that had graced the church. And in her own vision in song, the words were sung: "And when before the throne, I stand in him complete, 'Jesus died my soul to save,' my lips shall still repeat." What a perfect epitaph for the plain woman who had heard the voice of the Savior.

Beneath the Cross of Jesus

ELIZABETH C. CLEPHANE
1830 - 1869

FREDERICK C. MAKER
1844 - 1927

Beneath the cross of Jesus I fain would take my stand,
The shadow of a mighty Rock within a weary land;
A home within the wilderness, a rest upon the way,
From the burning of the noon-tide heat and the burden of the day.

Upon the cross of Jesus mine eye at times can see
The very dying form of One who suffered there for me:
And from my stricken heart with tears two wonders I confess,
The wonders of redeeming love and my unworthiness.

I take, O cross, thy shadow for my abiding place:
I ask no other sunshine than the sunshine of his face;
Content to let the world go by, to know no gain nor loss;
My sinful self my only shame, my glory all the cross.

AT THE HEART OF THE HYMN
Robert Wolgemuth

He will cover you with his feathers,

And under his wings you will find refuge.

—PSALM 91:4

$\mathcal{W}$HENEVER I THINK OF MY MOTHER'S DADDY—Grandpa Monroe Dourte—something happens to me. It's an indescribable combination of sadness and delight.

Now I know that Grandpa Dourte was human. His eight children have enough stories about this. Sometimes he had a temper—he *was* a redhead—and sometimes he sulked—he *was* a poet/musician. But by the time I met him, he had mostly worked through these things.

What I got was an incredible grandpa.

In the parlor at his house—a room that was not heated so my grandma could store freshly baked cookies for days—there was a huge, upright player piano. My brother Ken and I loved to dig through the stacks of large, perforated rolls in the closet that magically became music when we loaded them into the piano. "American Patrol" was my favorite. Ken liked "Whispering Hope."

Monroe Dourte played the harmonica to the delight of all of us (eight children and their spouses, thirty-five grandchildren and their spouses, over a hundred great-grandchildren and their spouses, and, at the time of his death in 1990, eight great-great grandchildren), his crystal blue eyes sparkling as he serenaded. He loved to sing. No one was ever concerned about covering the tenor part when he was around.

Grandpa was his own favorite comedian. He'd think of some clever saying or the first line of a hymn in German and sing it over and over again. *Yetscht der schvidt de vigh nocht sight. Yetscht der schvidt de vigh nocht sight.* I can still hear him giggle at himself. I had no idea what he had just said, but I'd laugh along.

As we walked the hundred or so feet from the kitchen screen door—the kind that didn't have any hydraulic brake, so it slammed shut with a loud smack—to his workshop and fired up the stove, he'd tell me stories about life on the farm and call me "Bobby." This city boy was thoroughly enchanted by the man.

"Daddy Dourte" knew God. (Considering it sacrilege, he winced when anyone would refer to him as "father.") When he prayed out loud, the timbre of his voice changed ever so slightly. You could tell that he was in the presence of someone he loved and deeply respected. And there was a hint of pleading in his words as he asked for God's mercy and protection for his family.

Grandpa Dourte was a self-taught biblical scholar. Thumbing through his Bible or his Sunday school notes tells its own story. Many passages were underlined. Handwritten notations packed the margins. And he had large portions committed to memory—especially the Psalms.

When our girls were five and eight, we went to visit Grandpa Dourte in the Pennsylvania rest home where he spent his final years. We listened to stories about farm life and sang hymns together. Our younger daughter, Julie, had memorized Psalm 91 and volunteered to recite it for Grandpa.

"He that dwelleth in the secret place of the Most High," Julie began, "shall abide under the shadow of the Almighty."

By the time she started the second verse, we were hearing the words in stereo. Grandpa Dourte was keeping pace with every word . . . "I will say of the LORD, He is my refuge and my fortress: my God; in him will I trust." Verse by verse, this little girl and her aged great-grandfather kept pace. "Thou shalt not be afraid . . . there shall no evil befall thee, neither shall any plague come nigh thy dwelling . . . with long life will I satisfy him, and show him my salvation."

We sang one more hymn together and hugged our good-byes after Grandpa offered a prayer of thanksgiving and blessing.

As our family left his room that afternoon, we paused in the hallway, just a few feet from Grandpa's door. We heard someone's voice. It sounded like Grandpa was speaking with someone. I looked around to see if one of the girls had lingered with him. But we were all accounted for.

We stopped to eavesdrop. Grandpa was talking to God. What we heard over the next few minutes was the most breathtaking conversation we had ever heard between a man and his heavenly Father.

Grandpa thanked the Lord for us—by name—and spoke another blessing on our family. Then he reminded the Father of his love for Him. When he was finished, we quietly walked down the hallway, through the lobby, to our car.

"You know," I said to Bobbie as we pulled out of the Messiah Village parking lot, "Grandpa's relationship with God is so intimate that he knows he's completely safe. That's the way he's always been. And even though he's facing his own imminent death, he's not afraid."

Grandpa's confidence was in God, his protection was sure, and his place was secure. And this gave him the freedom to step out of himself . . . to sing, to laugh, to worship, and to love others. I was one of the heirs of these good things.

I take, O cross, thy shadow for my abiding place:
I ask no other sunshine than the sunshine of his face . . .
And from my stricken heart with tears two wonders I confess,
The wonders of redeeming love and my unworthiness.

I don't suppose that I ever really thanked Grandpa Dourte for his love for me and his godly example. But that's okay. I'll have plenty of time to explain the whole thing to him when I see him again.

IN THE LIGHT OF THE WORD

John MacArthur

THIS PROFOUND EXPRESSION OF FAITH has been a favorite hymn for many generations. It is a pensive look at the significance of the cross, with particular emphasis on the amazing magnitude of Christ's love, set against the gross unworthiness of the ones for whom He died. In the words of the hymn's second stanza:

> *And from my stricken heart with tears*
> *Two wonders I confess,*
> *The wonders of redeeming love*
> *And my unworthiness.*

Stanza 1 evokes imagery from the Israelites' journey in the wilderness after they left Egypt and before they entered the Promised Land. God gave them water for that journey from a most unlikely source: a large rock. God told Moses, "'I will stand there before you by the rock at Horeb. Strike the rock, and water will come out of it for the people to drink.' So Moses did this in the sight of the elders of Israel" (Exodus 17:6).

Later in their wanderings, lacking water again, they encountered a rock once more. This time God told Moses, "Speak to that rock before their eyes and it will pour out its water. You will bring water out of the rock for the community so they and their livestock can drink" (Numbers 20:8). Unfortunately, Moses lost his temper and smote the rock twice. Nonetheless, "Water gushed out, and the community and their livestock drank" (v. 11).

That rock was a symbol of Christ, who provided spiritual refreshment for His people by being stricken. The apostle Paul wrote, "[Our forefathers] drank the same spiritual drink; for they drank from the spiritual rock that accompanied them, and that rock was Christ" (1 Corinthians 10:4).

The rock also symbolized the utter perfection of God. In the words of Moses, "He is the Rock, his works are perfect, and all his ways are just. A faithful God who does no wrong, upright and just is he" (Deuteronomy 32:4). Hannah prayed, "There is no one holy like the LORD; there is no one besides you; there is no Rock like our God" (1 Samuel 2:2). And the psalmist wrote, "The LORD is upright; he is my Rock, and there is no wickedness in him" (Psalm 92:15).

So the imagery of "a mighty Rock within a weary land" highlights the deity of Christ and the fact that He is the ultimate source of all our security, even though the blessings He bestows on His people flow from His being smitten on the cross. The hymn brilliantly captures the beauty of the biblical symbolism.

The closing stanza is a rich expression of faith and deep humility. It summarizes the whole theme of the hymn—that the cross provides all the shelter and sustenance we need for our difficult journey through this sinful, barren world.

The atoning work of Christ not only provides true shelter ("my abiding place") from the curse and consequences of our sin, but it also represents the source of true light ("I ask no other sunshine than the sunshine of his face"), the ground for true satisfaction ("Content to let the world go by, to know no gain nor loss"), and the only legitimate reason for true hope in the barrenness of our sinful world ("My sinful self my only shame, my glory all the cross").

Because it focuses so much on the worshiper's "unworthiness" and "shame," this hymn clearly harks back to an era before self-esteem was twisted into a "virtue." I love those expressions of personal contrition and deep humility. They are a fitting reminder that Scripture itself focuses on our sinfulness and says nothing whatsoever in favor of self-esteem. But as the hymn suggests, the cross is the true pinnacle of glory for the human race, because it was there that the sinless Son of God Himself, having taken on human form and lived a sinless life, redeemed us from our hopeless state of fallenness (cf. Galatians 6:14).

FROM OUT OF THE PAST

Bobbie Wolgemuth

*I*N A MALE-DOMINATED CHURCH CULTURE, women hymn-writers made a significant contribution of deeply heartfelt emotion in the form of verse. A delicate and frail young Scottish woman, Elizabeth Clephane, penned the words to this favorite Good Friday hymn.

Elizabeth came from a close family in Melrose, Scotland. Her father was a county sheriff and probably came home with stories of all the happenings of the townspeople—the pleasant and the pathetic. Perhaps that is why Elizabeth and her two sisters became rather famous in the area for serving the poor and sick. The girls did so much for charities—the disabled and the needy—that they gained a reputation for giving away everything except a meager bit to meet their own daily needs. They were resourceful in collecting the funds to carry on their work. Once they fell short and sold their own horse and carriage to meet the pressing demands of taking care of the poor.

Elizabeth was the youngest of the three girls and was spoken of as the "frail one" because of her poor health. Despite her physical limitations, however, her attitude was always cheerful, and the townspeople nicknamed her the "Sunbeam of Melrose."

In her young years, Elizabeth loved to write poetry. It was an outlet for express-ing her creative talent and giving voice to her deep spiritual side. It was also an acceptable occupation for a woman in early nineteenth-century Scotland. For both men and women in the Presbyterian Church of that day, it was said, "The Scots know their Bible!" This was certainly true of Elizabeth as she filled this Communion hymn with many images from both Old and New Testaments.

Bedridden and struggling with illness that would cause her early death at the young age of thirty-eight, Elizabeth continued to study Scripture and write intensely emotional verse. Expressing her own longings and hopes, and knowing she was on the very edge of life, the sense of submission is evident in her stanzas.

It is unmistakable that she was "content to let the world go by, to know no gain nor loss." Sadly, she never saw her hymns in print, as they were gathered and printed the year after her death in a Scottish Presbyterian publication entitled *Breathing on the Border*. She had asked in this hymn for "no other sunshine than the sunshine of his face," which is exactly what the "Sunbeam of Melrose" received for her reward.

The man who wrote the tune for this hymn had something in common with Elizabeth. They both served the poor and took no pleasure in worldly gain. Frederick Maker was an outstanding organist and composer who traveled exten-sively and played in English-speaking churches. He also gave concerts, many in poor areas of the towns where the people could not afford to pay him. He was known for taking whatever the underprivileged offered. On several occasions the concert organist ended up with sheep and a number of chickens for his pay-ment. Like Elizabeth, Frederick was rich in mercy and good works. He also knew the best was yet to come.

And Can It Be That I Should Gain

CHARLES WESLEY
1707-1788

And can it be that I should gain an int'rest in the Savior's blood?

Died he for me, who caused his pain?

For me, who him to death pursued?

Amazing love! How can it be that thou, my God, shouldst die for me?

Refrain:

Amazing love! How can it be

That thou, my God, shouldst die for me?

'Tis myst'ry all! Th'Immortal dies: who can explore his strange design?

In vain the first-born seraph tries

To sound the depths of love divine.

'Tis mercy all! Let earth adore, let angel minds inquire no more.

He left his Father's throne above (so free, so infinite his grace!),

Humbled himself (so great his love!),

And bled for all his chosen race.

'Tis mercy all, immense and free; for O, my God, it found out me.

Long my imprisoned spirit lay fast bound in sin and nature's night;

Thine eye diffused a quick'ning ray;

I woke, the dungeon flamed with light;

My chains fell off, my heart was free; I rose, went forth, and followed thee.

No condemnation now I dread; Jesus, and all in him, is mine!

Alive in him, my living Head,

And clothed in righteousness divine,

Bold I approach th'eternal throne, and claim the crown,

through Christ, my own.

At the Heart of the Hymn

Joni Eareckson Tada

. . . the exceeding riches of his grace, in his kindness toward us, through Christ Jesus.

—Ephesians 2:7, KJV

*H*AS THE MODERN ERA EVER PRODUCED a teenager who cared—really cared—about theology? The sort of theology they talk about in the dusty libraries of ivory towers? If you had asked me on November 13, 1964, I would have said "no." Great doctrines of the Christian faith were reserved for monks in robes or for seminary professors who kept their noses in the yellowed pages of thick textbooks.

My perspective changed, however, on November 14th. That morning as I sat on the hardwood floor of a camp meeting hall in Natural Bridge, Virginia, I felt my heart open to the Gospel being presented by our Young Life speaker. When he asked if any of us wanted to pray to embrace Christ as our Savior, I readily responded. That evening I found myself back at the camp meeting hall with the rest of my high school friends, clapping, singing, and celebrating my new birth into the family of God.

I noticed during the meeting that everything looked and felt different. The lights in the camp hall seemed brighter and warmer. The colors of my friends' clothes appeared more vivid, their smiles happier. Even the songs sounded different. Before, the hymns and gospel songs were fun to sing, but now they *meant* something. None was more striking than "And Can It Be." Especially the fourth verse.

Long my imprisoned spirit lay fast bound in sin
and nature's night;
Thine eye diffused a quick'ning ray;
I woke, the dungeon flamed with light;
My chains fell off, my heart was free;
I rose, went forth, and followed thee.

Everyone else continued singing, but I was mulling over the stanza. Twenty-four hours before, I would have given you a weird look had you told me my spirit lay imprisoned. Bound in sin? No way. But now with the Spirit of Christ residing inside me, I knew beyond a shadow of a doubt I had left behind "nature's night." It truly felt as though chains had fallen off.

This fact alone not only fascinated me, but plunged me into—what do you know—*theology*. I quickly learned that monks and professors were not the sole proprietors of the great doctrines of the Christian faith. In 2 Timothy 2:15 God encourages us *all* to "Study to show thyself approved unto God, a workman that needeth not to be ashamed, rightly dividing the word of truth" (KJV). And the more I studied, the more I appreciated the tight-knit biblical doctrine in every line of my favorite Young Life song, "And Can It Be."

Less than a month into my newfound faith in Christ, I had memorized all the stanzas. From then on, whenever I would sing it by heart at Wednesday night's Young Life Club, whenever I would hum it on the hockey field or whistle it in between classes, whenever it would swell inside my soul on a clear morning, whenever and wherever I happily sang all the stanzas, I was learning . . . great Christian doctrine.

And every time I sing it still, I become a better theologian.

IN THE LIGHT OF THE WORD

John MacArthur

E WERE BY NATURE OBJECTS OF WRATH. But because of his great love for us, God, who is rich in mercy, made us alive with Christ even when we were dead in transgressions" (Ephesians 2:3-5). "Christ died for the ungodly" (Romans 5:6). "God . . . justifies the wicked" (Romans 4:5). "God demonstrates his own love for us in this: While we were still sinners, Christ died for us" (Romans 5:8).

Those are amazing, ineffable truths. Words fail most of us when we attempt to express our awe and wonder over God's amazing love for sinners. But Charles Wesley has beautifully expressed it for us in this beloved hymn.

How can any sinner, whose sins were the cause of Christ's suffering, possibly deserve His mercy? How can we, people with hearts as evil as those who literally pursued the Savior to His death, expect to find forgiveness in Him? The answer is obvious: *In no sense* do we deserve His grace or merit His forgiveness. His amazing love is the *only* reason we partake of the benefits of His shed blood.

Christ's deity makes His death for sinners all the more staggering. Why would Someone who is God in human flesh stoop to die for unworthy sinners? And how could God incarnate, inherently immortal, die? As the second stanza says, this is a complete mystery—a "strange design." It is beyond human explanation. It overwhelms us with wonder.

By the way, Wesley was not suggesting that the eternal deity of Christ somehow perished on the cross ("that Thou, my God, shouldst die for me"; "Th' Immortal dies"). It was the *person* of Christ, the God-man, who died on the cross, not His deity or His humanity per se. Deity by definition *cannot* die. Yet Christ, the God-man, *did* die. No wonder Wesley refers to this doctrine as "myst'ry."

"The first-born seraph" in stanza 2 is a reference to Satan, who is portrayed in Ezekiel 28:13-17 as the highest of angels until he fell. According to the hymn, he tried in vain to exhaust the depths of divine love.

Stanza 3 rehearses the truth of Christ's self-humbling (Philippians 2:5-8)—leaving the Father's throne, humbling Himself, and dying. Wesley's original words spoke of Christ "emptying himself of all but love." I'm glad our version has slightly altered the words to make clear that Christ did not "empty Himself" of His other divine attributes. It is certain Wesley himself believed Christ retained His full deity, because he emphasizes the deity of Christ so much right here in this hymn, as well as throughout his hymnody. But more modern theologians have badly confused the issue, suggesting that Christ's self-emptying (Philippians 2:7) involved the abandonment of His deity. We know from Scripture that Christ gave up none of the essence of deity.

Stanza 4 is a beautiful personal testimony about the sinner's awakening from his state of spiritual death. Notice that God's grace precedes and enables the sinner's movement toward God. The Spirit of God first enlivens and awakens him ("thine eye diffused a quick'ning ray"). He is freed from the chains of sin, and then he responds in faith ("I rose, went forth, and followed thee"). That is the proper biblical order. Unless God had first freed us from the bondage of sin and drawn us to Christ, none of us would have ever believed (John 6:44, 65).

The final stanza is surely one of the hymnbook's finest poetic statements about justification by faith. It begins with a reference to Romans 8:1: "There is now no condemnation for those who are in Christ Jesus." It also refers to the headship of Christ, spoken of in 1 Corinthians 11:3; Ephesians 1:22; 4:15; 5:23; Colossians 1:18; 2:19. "Clothed in righteousness divine" is an allusion to Isaiah 61:10, one of the great Old Testament texts about justification: "The LORD . . . has clothed me with garments of salvation and arrayed me in a robe of righteousness."

The closing line is an echo of Hebrews 4:16: "Let us then approach the throne of grace with confidence, so that we may receive mercy and find grace to help us in our time of need."

FROM OUT OF THE PAST
Bobbie Wolgemuth

*I*T IS FROM THE CRUCIBLE OF THREE DRAMATIC experiences that the celebrated Methodist reformer Charles Wesley wrote this Easter hymn. The first was his agony on a storm-tossed ship; the second, his sudden healing from a severe illness; and the third, the conversion of a slave shortly before execution.

Charles was twenty-nine years old and returning from Georgia to England when a mighty hurricane arose in the Atlantic. For several days the violent sea washed into the vessel and swept away most of the sheep and other livestock on board. The sailors desperately attempted to bail water and keep the ship afloat. Charles was too shaken to pray but made himself repeat the name of Jesus over and over until he was able to lift his voice in prayer. Calling for faith in Jesus, he finally felt assurance that he was "under the shadow of the Almighty." The storm still swirling around them, Charles began to encourage the other passengers. When the captain cut the mast, finding it impossible to save the ship, Charles was hopeful and continued to pray with the others. In his journal Charles recorded that "toward morning the sea heard and obeyed the divine voice." The experience would find its way into word pictures in later hymns.

The second experience was the dramatic transformation that gripped the body and soul of Charles when he was lodging in an upstairs room in London. Feeling desperately ill with a fever and struggling to breathe, Charles had an apparition of a woman who spoke to him. Her words were, "In the name of Jesus of Nazareth arise, and believe, and thou shalt be healed of all thy infirmities." When she faded away, Charles called down to find her and was told that no one had been there. He immediately opened up his Bible and was enveloped with a new assurance of Christ's amazing love. His brother John reported that "his bodily strength returned from that very hour." This experience set an evangelistic fire in Charles's soul that never faded.

The third experience was in July 1838 when Charles was thirty-one years old. With new boldness and a calling to reach the poor and outcasts of society he had gone to Newgate, the infamous London prison, to preach. It was a cruel penitentiary where men, especially slaves, were condemned for the most minor offenses. Hangings were conducted for townspeople to view like sporting events.

Charles took a special interest in a poor African slave condemned to hang for stealing from his master. The hopeless man listened with astonishment as Charles told him about Christ who came from heaven to die an agonizing death just for him. Tears streamed down his black cheeks, and his heart was changed, along with the hearts of several other prisoners. The next week, on the day of execution, Charles prayed and sang hymns with the men as they were loaded onto a cart, their hands tied behind their backs.

Charles reported later, "I never saw such calm triumph, such incredible indifference to dying." They sang several hymns together before the cart drew off. The newly converted prisoners never stirred or struggled for life but meekly gave up their spirits. Charles recorded in his journal, "That hour under the gallows was the most blessed hour of my life." The sight of redeemed men going to their death with composed countenance was translated into the passionate stanza, "No condemnation now I dread; Jesus, and all in him, is mine!"

An intricate tapestry of Scripture and dramatic vignettes drawn from these life-changing experiences, this Easter hymn is one of Charles Wesley's most beloved works.

Jesus, Thy Blood and Righteousness

NIKOLAUS LUDWIG
VON ZINZENDORF
1700-1760

Jesus, thy blood and righteousness my beauty are, my glorious dress;
'Midst flaming worlds, in these arrayed, with joy shall I lift up my head.

Bold shall I stand in thy great day; for who aught to my charge shall lay?
Fully absolved through these I am from sin and fear,
from guilt and shame.

When from the dust of death I rise to claim my mansion in the skies,
E'en then this shall be all my plea, Jesus hath lived, hath died, for me.

Jesus, be endless praise to thee, whose boundless mercy hath for me—
For me a full atonement made, an everlasting ransom paid.

O let the dead now hear thy voice; now bid thy banished ones rejoice;
Their beauty this, their glorious dress, Jesus, thy blood and righteousness.

AT THE HEART OF THE HYMN
Robert Wolgemuth

See how the lilies of the field grow. They do not labor or spin. Yet I tell you that not even Solomon in all his splendor was dressed like one of these.

—MATTHEW 6:28B-29

*N*OT UNTIL OUR DAUGHTERS WERE BORN did I have any idea what clothing meant.

Growing up in a large family and being the third son, I learned to live with hand-me-downs. Fortunately, most of the things I got were only second-generation—not that there was anything wrong with the way my oldest brother, Sam, wore his clothes. It's just that if things had to go through all three of us, their mileage was much more visible, if you know what I mean.

Sweaters, jackets, and sport coats were the most likely candidates to see more than one owner during their lifetimes. Because our mother was adept at a sewing machine and could put a patch on anything, sometimes play clothes also found themselves with a rich history of Sam, Ken, and Robert. (Our fourth brother, Dan, came along eight years later, and as I recall, he was the inaugural owner of most of his clothes.)

But none of this was a problem. We were boys. Clothing was clothing. You get up in the morning, jump into whatever you're wearing that day, and it's on to the next thing. What you have on simply doesn't cross your mind until it's time to take if off at the end of the day.

Of course, as we grew up, clothing *did* take on greater importance. As teenagers, my brothers took jobs as clerks in a local haberdashery. At fourteen or fifteen, I found myself interested in girls; so my clothing went to the next level, too.

Eight years later I was married, and two years after that I held our first daughter in my arms. I had no experience with little girls but figured my track record of growing up as a boy—and hanging around my brothers—would put me in a good position to know what it would be like to raise a girl. After all, a kid is a kid.

Color me dead wrong.

Not only was this little girl—and the sister that followed her three years later—different than a boy, I soon discovered that there was *nothing* in my own experience as a kid that would be of any help at all. And one of the areas that was completely new for me was this thing about clothing. I had no idea.

I don't want to exaggerate here, but some mornings the girls would get dressed two or three times before leaving the house. Sometimes more.

Early-morning discussions—arguments—with their mother were often the reason for the outfit changes. I was sailing in uncharted water. Our daughters weren't being bratty; it's just that I was accustomed to going off to school wearing Ken's sweater and Sam's jacket. For a girl, clothing wasn't just clothing. Outfits actually *meant* something.

Now that our daughters are adults, our photo albums chronicle the transitions from one clothing stage to the next. Sometimes when we're together we look at the albums and laugh at the styles they wore.

But there's one photo album that's not funny at all.

On September 24, 1994 and July 31, 1999 our daughters put on wedding dresses. I stood back and drank it all in. The memory still takes my breath away. And those dresses changed everything. From that moment on, they belonged to someone new. Sure, I was still their daddy, but now they loved another man with a greater love.

Even more than when they were in grade school or junior high, what they wore that day really meant something.

Whether you're a man or a woman, you and I have an outfit that makes a fashion statement unlike anything mankind has ever known.

Jesus, thy blood and righteousness
My beauty are,
My glorious dress.

The cross of Christ—His loving sacrifice—gave us a new suit of clothes. Now by faith we can stand before the bridegroom, a holy and perfect God, forgiven and beautiful beyond description.

You are all sons of God through faith in Christ Jesus, for all of you who were baptized into Christ have been clothed with Christ.
—GALATIANS 3:26-27

My brothers and I were wrong. Our girls were right. Clothes really *do* mean something.

IN THE LIGHT OF THE WORD
John MacArthur

COUNT NIKOLAUS LUDWIG VON ZINZENDORF was the leader of the Moravian Brethren, noted for their strong emphasis on practical personal piety and missionary work. But this classic hymn is not about the believer's subjective devotion to Christ; it is about the objective grounds of every true Christian's justification: the righteousness of Christ and His atoning work on our behalf. This is a fine doctrinal hymn about the believer's justification by faith alone.

The hymn-writer recognizes that personal piety is *not* what gives believers a righteous standing before God. The only "beauty" and "glorious dress" that we have in God's sight are the pure and perfect righteousness of Christ, imputed to us through faith. That imputed righteousness encompasses what theologians sometimes refer to as His *active obedience* (the perfect obedience Jesus rendered to the Mosaic law in His earthly life) and His *passive obedience* (His death on the cross). Hence the shorthand of "blood" (referring to Christ's passive obedience) "and righteousness" (referring to His active obedience).

Zinzendorf lived in an era when the world was troubled by much turmoil and strife. When he speaks of "flaming worlds," he is describing life as he knew it in the early eighteenth century. He was an extremely wealthy nobleman whose travels took him all over Europe, to England, and even to America. Zinzendorf witnessed tremendous political and social upheaval, and he suffered persecution for his faith in all those places. But he confesses that as long as He is clothed ("arrayed") in Christ's perfect righteousness, he can lift up his head with joy in *any* earthly circumstance. That is a healthy view of justification. And it is as relevant amid the "flaming worlds" of today as it was in Zinzendorf's time.

The second stanza speaks of the Christian's boldness in the day of judgment. The apostle John wrote, "We will have confidence on the day of judgment, because in this world we are like him" (1 John 4:17). We are "like him" primarily in the sense that we are clothed in His perfect righteousness and "fully absolved" from any guilt. "Therefore, there is now no condemnation for those who are in Christ Jesus" (Romans 8:1). The second line of the stanza echoes Romans 8:33: "Who will bring any charge against those whom God has chosen? It is God who justifies." No one—including Satan, the accuser of the brethren (Revelation 12:10)—can charge believers with guilt in the court of God, because Christ has already atoned for all their sins.

Stanza 3 acknowledges that even in the resurrection ("When from the dust of death I rise"), the believer's only plea as he stands before God will be that "Jesus hath lived" (referring again to His active obedience) and "hath died" (a reference to His passive obedience) "for me." In other words, He lived His perfect life and died that awful death in our place, as our Substitute. And that is the *only* reason we can stand before God without fear of condemnation.

Even in the final judgment, not one aspect of our justification before God will stem from any good thing *we* have done—even the good works God graciously empowers and enables us to do (cf. Ephesians 2:10). The sole ground of our justification is what Christ has done *for* us.

It is noteworthy that Zinzendorf, whose Moravian Brethren placed so much stress on the importance of good works, has nonetheless so strongly emphasized here that justification is by faith alone because of Christ's righteousness alone. The hymn reflects an accurate, biblical view of justification by faith.

Stanza 4 is an expression of praise to Christ, acknowledging that He has already made "a full atonement" and paid an "everlasting ransom." Again, this stresses that the work of our salvation is done. There is nothing we must add to it. All *our* works of righteousness are merely the outworking of Christ's finished work. Our justification is a settled fact (Romans 5:1), grounded in Christ's work alone.

The closing stanza completes the hymn with a prayer of expectation and longing for the day when the dead shall rise to eternal glory. Even then, the hymn-writer suggests, their sole "beauty" and "glorious dress" will be the imputed righteousness of the Savior.

FROM OUT OF THE PAST
Bobbie Wolgemuth

AS A LITTLE BOY, NIKOLAUS LUDWIG heard stories of great men driven by conviction to battle for their faith. Born into a wealthy and influential German family, he was raised by his grandmother who guarded his education at school and university to be exclusively part of the grassroots reformation called Pietism. His godfather, Philipp Spener, was a pastor and founder of the Pietistic movement. A devout believer, he encouraged small groups of people to gather in homes to stir their souls by hymn-singing, prayer, and discussions about personal faith.

Nikolaus listened to Spener and his comrades tell of heroes of the past like John Hus who had suffered martyrdom in the fifteenth century for their Christian beliefs. With great composure and even joy, these persecuted saints had quoted the Apostles' Creed and had sung Easter hymns as the flames enveloped them. The stories captured both the heart and resolve of young von Zinzendorf.

Nikolaus studied law at the University of Wittenberg and, after extensive travel, returned home to become Counselor of State at the court of Saxony, all the while maintaining his youthful passion for prayer meetings, hymn singing, and hymn-writing. His godfather showed him, by example, to use his contacts in person and correspondence to influence the whole church to move from spiritual poverty to "Christianity of the heart."

When Count von Zinzendorf was twenty-two, a tiny band of Moravian Christians fled persecution to safety on his extensive estate in Saxony. These hunted men had heard of a nobleman named Zinzendorf who had a reputation for being hospitable to oppressed people. They brought with them their ancient German hymnbook. This gave Nikolaus the opportunity he had long sought to develop a "true church," using the hymns and sharing the devotion to cultivate deep faith and fellowship. Preparation and vision met as the young nobleman became the inspirer, organizer, and hymn poet of the Moravian Brethren.

The tiny group built a village on his large estate, which they named "Herrnhut," meaning "the Lord's shelter." For ten years additional refugees came, and soon they numbered over 600. Facing growing opposition from the state church, Nikolaus encouraged the band of believers to send missionaries to the

West Indies and America. The zeal and heroism of the missionaries was extraordinary as they evangelized and organized the converts.

Nikolaus wrote hundreds of hymns, editing and publishing Moravian hymnbooks constantly. These hymnbooks were taken all over the world and proved to be the most potent weapon in the missionary arsenal. One of the hymnbooks fell into the hands of a man who would change church history in Europe, John Wesley. On a voyage to Georgia, it was the singing of the Moravians that inspired Wesley to teach and write hymns. Wesley studied German in order to translate the hymns he heard into English. This became the driving force behind Methodism.

John Wesley translated "Jesus, Thy Blood and Righteousness" from Zinzendorf's hymnal in 1740, the year after it was written. It was set to a tune called "Germany," which moves and swells with strength, honoring the Moravian brethren who lived "'midst flaming worlds" with confidence.

Daring to go where others feared to tread marked the life of Count von Zinzendorf. Inspiring his followers with music, he wrote over two thousand hymns before his death at age sixty. The stories of courage and calling he had heard as a young boy were the characteristics that marked his life. With a passion for Christ and a hymnbook in his hand, he left wide footsteps for us to follow. In his own words from the Easter hymn he composed, his epitaph could be, "Bold shall I stand in thy great day."

Jesus, Keep Me Near the Cross

FANNY CROSBY
1820-1915

WILLIAM H. DOANE
1832-1915

Jesus, keep me near the cross; there a precious fountain,
Free to all—a healing stream—flows from Calv'ry's mountain.

Refrain:
In the cross, in the cross, be my glory ever;
Till my raptured soul shall find rest beyond the river.

Near the cross, a trembling soul, love and mercy found me;
There the Bright and Morning Star shed its beams around me.

Near the cross! O Lamb of God, bring its scenes before me;
Help me walk from day to day with its shadow o'er me.

Near the cross I'll watch and wait, hoping, trusting ever,
Till I reach the golden strand just beyond the river.

AT THE HEART OF THE HYMN

Joni Eareckson Tada

God forbid that I should glory, save in the cross of our Lord Jesus Christ.

—GALATIANS 6:14, KJV

ANGRY, SULLEN, AND STUBBORNLY RESISTANT against God and His will—this described me to a T in the late sixties. After the classic stages of shock, bargaining, and denial, I was now in the anger phase. I hated the idea of living the rest of my life as a quadriplegic.

On the other hand, I hated the loneliness and depression. I desperately wanted "out," but I was clueless as to where to begin. I needed to know the shortest route to peace and hope. I needed rest. Rest from the hot, seething emotions that constantly had me in tears. Somewhere in between boxes of Kleenex, I stumbled across this hymn. The words seemed way too simple:

Jesus, keep me near the cross; there a precious fountain,
Free to all—a healing stream—flow from Calv'ry's mountain.
In the cross, in the cross, be my glory ever;
Till my raptured soul shall find rest beyond the river.

I scowled. *Bear a cross? I hate the idea of taking up your cross daily. What's the cross got to do with it?* A friend, Steve Estes, bore the brunt of my prickly questions. "If you want to know what the cross has to do with your situation," he countered, "I suggest we start with Philippians 3:10, 'That I may know him, and the power of his resurrection, and the fellowship of his sufferings, being made conformable unto his death'" (KJV).

Huh? was all over my face.

"Joni, do you want to know Christ?" I nodded a halfhearted "yes."

"And the power of His resurrection?" Power was something I knew I needed, and so again I said, "Yes."

"And the fellowship of sharing in His sufferings?" I wasn't too sure about that. "Becoming like Him in his death?"

At this point, Steve was off my radar screen. I answered, "Who wants to become like Christ in His death? Anyway, I don't even know what that means."

It was then that Steve gave me a quick lesson in *Christian Growth 101*. I learned that to become like Christ in His death means to die *to* the sins He died *for.* It means to take up my cross just like He took up His. In so doing, I would become like Him in His death as I put anger and resentment behind me. And frankly—Steve told me—it would take the power of the resurrection to die to the sorts of sins that had so long gripped my heart.

"If you want peace, hope, and rest," Steve said, "then you have to lay that load of resentment at the foot of the cross. Once you become like Christ in His death, *then you fully experience His life!*"

It was just the answer I needed. Over the years I would see that the cross *is* the power of God. It is there He confides in those who fear Him. It's at the cross where you can find the secret things that belong to the Lord. It is there you are sorrowful, yet always rejoicing; having nothing, yet possessing everything (2 Corinthians 6:10). It is at the cross where all things are yours and "you are of Christ, and Christ is of God" (1 Corinthians 3:23). At the foot of the cross you find peace and rest.

Somehow God stood my suffering on its head and used it like a jackhammer to break apart my rocks of resistance. God turned it upside down and used it to sandblast me to the core; although I was left bare, I could then be bonded to the Savior. "And remember," Steve concluded, "your wheelchair may end up being your ally. It can be the sheepdog that snaps at your heels, forcing you down the road to Calvary, forcing you to stay near the cross."

It's been many years since those early days when Steve took me down the road to Calvary. I left anger in the dust decades ago, but hardly a day goes by that I don't remember . . . that I don't thank God . . . and sing—not with a scowl but a smile—"Jesus, keep me near the cross!"

IN THE LIGHT OF THE WORD
John MacArthur

 AUL'S WORDS IN GALATIANS 6:14 ("May I never boast except in the cross of our Lord Jesus Christ, through which the world has been crucified to me, and I to the world") have been the basis for a number of familiar hymns, but none more beloved than this simple yet profound setting by Fanny Crosby.

The first stanza speaks of "a healing stream" that flows "free to all" from "a precious fountain" on Calvary. The imagery in the hymn is a reference to the "water of life" mentioned in Revelation 22:17: "The Spirit and the bride say, 'Come!' And let him who hears say, 'Come!' Whoever is thirsty, let him come; and whoever wishes, let him take the free gift of the water of life."

Jesus employed similar terms when He spoke to the Samaritan woman at Jacob's well. He said, "Whoever drinks the water I give him will never thirst. Indeed, the water I give him will become in him a spring of water welling up to eternal life" (John 4:14).

Only Christ's atoning work on the cross could have made possible the granting of life to sinners. The true living water therefore "flows from Calv'ry's mountain." The words of the hymn trace the living stream back to its source, pleading with the Savior to keep us there, "near the cross," close to the precious fountain itself.

The second stanza is a verse of personal testimony. Symbolically, the foot of the cross is the ground on which all sinners are saved. First, they recognize their own sin and unworthiness. That realization produces "a trembling soul." But then light breaks as "the Bright and Morning Star" embraces the sinner with blood-bought forgiveness.

That name for Christ is borrowed from Revelation 22:16, where Jesus Himself says, "I am the Root and the Offspring of David, and the bright Morning Star." The name echoes one of the earliest biblical prophecies of the Messiah, found in Numbers 24:17, where Moses promised the Israelites, "A star will come out of Jacob; a scepter will rise out of Israel" (cf. Luke 1:78; 2 Peter 1:19).

Stanza 3 shows the relevance of the cross to the believer's daily life. It reminds us that the Christian is supposed to "walk from day to day" in the footsteps of Christ—footsteps that lead each one to "deny himself and take up his cross and follow" (Matthew 16:24). Thus the Christian life is to be lived in the shadow of the cross, following the One who "'committed no sin, and no deceit was found in his mouth.' When they hurled their insults at him, he did not retaliate; when he suffered, he made no threats. Instead, he entrusted himself to him who judges justly" (1 Peter 2:22-23).

That is the true path of holiness as described in Scripture. The hymn-writer thus reminds us that not only our justification, but also our sanctification is grounded in the work of Christ on the cross.

The closing stanza looks forward to heavenly glory, when we "reach the golden strand just beyond the river." "The river" is familiar symbolism referring to death, which ushers us into the glory of heaven. In the meantime, we "watch and wait, hoping, trusting ever"—with our hearts fixed on the glory of the cross.

It is a dramatic paradox to say as Paul did, and as the hymn-writer echoes, that the Christian's glory is only in the cross. From a worldly perspective, the cross would seem to symbolize the very opposite of glory. It was, of course, a symbol of death, disgrace, and dishonor—the antithesis of what we usually think of when we think of "glory." But as Christians, we know that we have nothing to boast about or glory in, except what Christ accomplished on our behalf at Calvary. The cross therefore symbolizes our only true glory. And even when our "raptured soul[s] shall find rest beyond the river," the cross will continue to be the one true token of our hope and glory.

From Out of the Past
Bobbie Wolgemuth

GIFTED WITH A PHENOMENAL MIND and rare sensitivity, the blind poetess Fanny Crosby was called a "sweet singer in the night." Frances Jane Crosby was born to a godly couple in New York City. And it's a tribute to their entire family how they transformed the tragic circumstances that took their baby girl from sight to blindness when she was a tiny six-month-old.

A mistaken poultice put on her eyes by a man filling in for the town doctor caused baby Frances to lose all sight except the ability to distinguish light from darkness. But instead of harboring bitterness toward the misguided man posing as a doctor, Fanny's parents and grandmother devoted themselves to helping her overcome her disability and fulfill God's calling on her life.

A happy and confident youngster, Fanny could dress herself, climb trees, and ride horses bareback. She was determined to accomplish almost anything sighted children could do.

When she was only eight years old Fanny was already displaying the cheerful disposition and winsome gift of poetry that marked her life.

Oh, what a happy soul am I!
Although I cannot see,
I am resolved that in this world
Contented I will be.

How many blessings I enjoy
That other people don't;
To weep and sigh because I'm blind,
I cannot, and I won't.

Her grandmother took Fanny on long walks and would describe in meticulous detail the treasures in nature they found on the way. Recognizing her thirst for knowledge, her grandmother also spent hours every day reading great literature, poetry, and Scripture to the little girl. By the time she was ten years old, this gifted child had memorized all four Gospels, the Pentateuch, many of the Psalms, Proverbs, Ruth, and the Song of Solomon.

Her patient and dedicated grandmother taught Fanny to pray on her knees from a tender age. With no schools equipped to instruct blind children, they knelt beside her grandmother's rocking chair and specifically asked God to provide a way for Fanny to learn "like the other children." The answer came when she was twelve with an opportunity to attend the New York Institute for the Blind. There she excelled as the top student, studying music, literature, history, and languages, as well as becoming accomplished in playing the guitar, harp, piano, and organ. Years later, while a teacher at the Institute, Fanny was overwhelmed when more than half of her beloved students died from a severe cholera epidemic in 1849. Kneeling in prayer at a local revival, Fanny asked God to change her heart and to give her assurance of her own place in heaven. The God of her grandmother answered her prayer with a radical conversion and a new calling on her life.

From that time on, Fanny felt called to hymn-writing and mission work. Her passion was that her life would be the means of leading one million souls to Christ. On the streets of the New York Bowery, carrying her Bible and a little American flag, she would sympathetically care for the derelicts she called "her boys" several days each week. She said it was the most wonderful work in the world and commented that the one thing all people want is love. Fanny had a full measure of such devotion and dished it out generously with music, poetry, and humor.

Fanny considered her blindness a gift and with charm told her admirers that she was anticipating her Savior to be the first face to gladden her sight. When asked how she felt about the imposter who caused her to lose her sight, Fanny described her gratefulness for the means by which she was consecrated for her lifework. Wearing dark rectangular glasses, telling whimsical stories, and quoting poetry she had composed, she could light up a room with her great talent, wit, and charisma.

The composer of the melody for "Jesus, Keep Me Near the Cross" was a successful businessman and humble benefactor. William Doane, while president of a manufacturing company, generously volunteered time and money to church and civic activities. His creative mind was the genius behind more than seventy inventions, while music was an avocation for him that flourished as much as his woodworking machinery business. He composed over two thousand hymn tunes as well as editing and publishing over forty hymn collections. William admired

Fanny's creative mind and shared her passion for mission work. He wrote several tunes for her poems including "Rescue the Perishing" and "To God Be the Glory."

Fanny never began her work without asking the Lord to be her inspiration. Often a minister would tell her what his sermon topic would be at an upcoming service. She would listen, go into her room, pray, then compose a song in her head before dictating the verses to her secretary. That evening the hymn would be sung as a prelude to the sermon. In the same way, musicians would play their tunes for Fanny. With lines coming to her as fast as they could be copied, sometimes she would remark, "This is what I hear the tune saying."

Fanny Crosby died at age ninety-five. Of the more than nine thousand hymns she had written in her lifetime, the one played at her funeral service stated, "And I shall see Him face to face and tell the story—saved by grace." And on a simple headstone bearing the name "Aunt Fanny" is written "Blessed assurance, Jesus is mine. Oh, what a foretaste of glory divine."

There Is a Fountain Filled with Blood

WILLIAM COWPER
1731-1800

LOWELL MASON
1792-1872

There is a fountain filled with blood, drawn from Immanuel's veins;
And sinners, plunged beneath that flood, lose all their guilty stains:
Lose all their guilty stains, lose all their guilty stains,
And sinners, plunged beneath that flood, lose all their guilty stains.

The dying thief rejoiced to see that fountain in his day;
And there have I, as vile as he, washed all my sins away:
Washed all my sins away, washed all my sins away;
And there have I, as vile as he, washed all my sins away.

E'er since by faith I saw the stream your flowing wounds supply,
Redeeming love has been my theme, and shall be till I die:
And shall be till I die, and shall be till I die;
Redeeming love has been my theme, and shall be till I die.

Then in a nobler, sweeter song I'll sing your pow'r to save,
When this poor lisping, stamm'ring tongue lies silent in the grave:
Lies silent in the grave, lies silent in the grave;
When this poor lisping, stamm'ring tongue lies silent in the grave.

Dear dying Lamb, your precious blood shall never lose its pow'r,
Till all the ransomed church of God be saved to sin no more:
Be saved to sin no more, be saved to sin no more;
Till all the ransomed church of God be saved to sin no more.

AT THE HEART OF THE HYMN

Joni Eareckson Tada

"On that day a fountain will be opened to the house of David and the inhabitants of Jerusalem, to cleanse them from sin and impurity."

—ZECHARIAH 13:1

W HEN I WAS GROWING UP—the youngest of four sisters—my daddy painted three beautiful angels on the slanted wall of my bedroom. Lying in bed, I'd stare at all three oil-painted cherubs singing with their mouths open like big O's and holding sheet music with their feet firmly planted in the clouds. The first angel looked like my oldest sister Linda with brown hair. The angel in the middle had a thick tousle of blonde curls. I guessed that was Jay Kay.

Jay was my favorite angel. And my favorite sister. A teenager in the fifties, she was a few years younger than Linda and so liked Elvis less for "Jailhouse Rock" and more for "Let Me Be Your Teddy Bear." Jay looked like Betty, the fair-haired girl with the pony tail in the *Archie* comics, or, when she wore her hair down, like Daisy Mae in the comic strip *L'il Abner*. She didn't treat me like a tagalong. She liked me. "Jonathan Grundy," she would affectionately call me. When Jay played "Sentimental Journey" on our upright piano, I tried to mimic her. When she would sing, I would chime in. When she sewed skirts, I gave it a try. When she artfully messed with her hair, I twisted mine up. I couldn't understand why Bob Barker didn't want her as Miss Maryland for the Miss America Pageant.

Jay Kay must have known how much I looked up to her. Maybe that's why, many years later in the early seventies after the diving accident in which I became paralyzed, she asked me to come live with her. There was lots of room in the old stone house up on the farm.

Ahh, the farm. And, ah, my sister Jay. I was still a novice at being a quadriplegic, struggling to adjust to my wheelchair, but my older sibling made the early years of adapting to paralysis bearable. Sometimes even sweet.

Jay was the one behind the fresh, crisp sheets and the coffee and sizzling bacon in the morning. She'd set her five-year-old, Jayme, on the edge of my bed to teach her how to count out my "stretching" exercises. We'd swap clothes, try new recipes, bake cookies, and lead Brownie troops together. In the afternoon Jay would set up my painting easel and arrange my pencils. In the evening it'd be a Bible study with friends or we'd keep our drinks hot by the hearth and listen to John Denver. I knew my spirits were improving when, from our farmhouse window, I could watch my sister saddle up, wave to me from the barn, and be content to see her enjoy a horseback ride on a brisk fall day.

To help my friends feel at home around my new wheelchair, Jay would invite them to stay for dinner. She'd spread gingham over the large farmhouse table, light the candles, and set out generous bowls of steaming corn and asparagus from her garden, with the best hot-baked potatoes this side of Idaho and hamburgers that made your mouth water. After dessert we'd pull our chairs around the fire and sing until midnight. To this day whenever I run into friends who came up to the farm, they still get a dreamy look, smile, and say wistfully, "Never were there better days than those times at Jay's house. My favorite memories are those nights on the farm."

And my favorite memory? There are many, but I remember best that late summer evening on the back porch under a full moon when Jay pulled up her rocker. There, with crickets calling under the willow and fireflies floating over the creek, with moonlight on her golden hair, we lifted our voices on this old hymn . . .

There is a fountain filled with blood,
Drawn from Immanuel's veins;

And sinners, plunged beneath that flood,
Lose all their guilty stains:
Lose all their guilty stains, lose all their guilty stains;
And sinners, plunged beneath that flood,
Lose all their guilty stains.

We didn't need a dulcimer. We didn't need a fiddle. I slid my harmony underneath her melody as our voices—soft as country down—blended into the night, making our praises to God as sweet as honeysuckle.

I owe so much to my sister. More than I can say. At the most fragile time of my life, she stood by me, cajoling and coaxing me out of depression with gingham, grace, and a friendship that only sisters share. There is much that binds us together. It's the same binding you can hear on tight country harmony on an old hymn.

Years have passed since those days on the farm, but still, when Jay and I get together, we almost always launch into that favorite family hymn. And when we hit the high notes, I'm back at that soft summer night on the porch, watching my sister's long blonde hair swing in rhythm with the rocker. It was the night we sang with no sheet music, like angels with our feet firmly planted in the clouds.

IN THE LIGHT OF THE WORD
John MacArthur

ZECHARIAH 13:1 SAYS, "A fountain will be opened to the house of David and the inhabitants of Jerusalem, to cleanse them from sin and impurity." Hymnwriter William Cowper combined that imagery with the truth of 1 John 1:7:

"The blood of Jesus . . . purifies us from every sin." The result is a hymn whose language is shockingly vivid. It reminds us that the price of our cleansing and forgiveness from sin was nothing less than the very lifeblood of God's Son, poured out for us on the cross.

Blood was a key symbol in the Old Testament sacrificial system. Leviticus 17:11 says, "The life of a creature is in the blood, and I have given it to you to make atonement for yourselves on the altar; it is the blood that makes atonement for one's life."

When Moses instituted the Law, according to Exodus 24:1-8, he collected the blood of several animal sacrifices in some large basins. Then, using a broomlike shrub called hyssop, he spattered the blood all over the tabernacle, its furnishings, and the people of Israel.

Hebrews 9:19-22 describes the awful scene:

> When Moses had proclaimed every commandment of the law to all the people, he took the blood of calves, together with water, scarlet wool and branches of hyssop, and sprinkled the scroll and all the people. He said, "This is the blood of the covenant, which God has commanded you to keep." In the same way, he sprinkled with the blood both the tabernacle and everything used in its ceremonies. In fact, the law requires that nearly everything be cleansed with blood.

And the writer of Hebrews added, "Without the shedding of blood there is no forgiveness."

The blood sacrifices graphically showed that atonement for sin required an extremely high price. The blood of an innocent victim had to be shed to pay the price.

But the Old Testament sacrifices were merely symbolic, "because it is impossible for the blood of bulls and goats to take away sins" (Hebrews 10:4). Only a perfect human could pay the price for human sins. That is why the eternal Son of God humbled Himself and took on human form (vv. 5-10).

The animal sacrifices merely symbolized and foreshadowed the blood that would be shed by the perfect sacrifice, Jesus Christ. His bloody death on the cross was the only *real* atonement for sins ever offered, the perfect sacrifice for sins offered once for all and forever. "He did not enter by means of the blood of goats and calves; but he entered the Most Holy Place once for all by his own blood, having obtained eternal redemption" (Hebrews 9:12).

In Scripture, the expression *the blood of Christ* is rich with meaning. It evokes the idea of literal bloodshed, to be sure—but the primary reference is to the *death* of Christ, not merely His wounds. If He had only bled without dying, the price of atonement would not have been met.

Scripture is full of these expressions: "It was not with perishable things such as silver or gold that you were redeemed from the empty way of life handed down to you from your forefathers, but with the precious blood of Christ" (1 Peter 1:18-19). "[Christ] loves us and has freed us from our sins by his blood" (Revelation 1:5). "In him we have redemption through his blood, the forgiveness of sins, in accordance with the riches of God's grace" (Ephesians 1:7). Again and again Scripture emphasizes that the price of redemption was nothing less than the very life of Christ, poured out through the shedding of His blood.

The words of this hymn should always be sung thoughtfully. It paints a picture many people find disturbing. But it is nonetheless gloriously true that the price of our redemption was blood "drawn from Immanuel's veins."

Shocking? Yes. But far from being appalled by it, we ought to fall on our faces with gratitude and amazement that Jesus Christ, the Lamb of God, was willing to pay such a horrible price to provide eternal life for undeserving sinners.

From Out of the Past

Bobbie Wolgemuth

A RESPECTED ENGLISH POET, William Cowper struggled with ill health and depression much of his adult life. His mother, being from a well-known family of royalty, exposed young William to the finest literature and verse from her family's extensive library. The close relationship he had with her ended with her untimely death when he was only six years old. He clung to her memory and her love for poetry even though his clergyman father pushed him to study law.

Despite extraordinary success in studies and writing, not a day passed that William did not mourn the death of his beloved mother. His first mental breakdown came as a result of anxiety over an examination for a clerkship in the House of Lords. His failed attempts at suicide by poison, stabbing, and hanging led to his detention in St. Alban's asylum. There his brother visited him and brought the healing message of salvation. At the age of thirty-three, William was converted, and his mental and spiritual restoration began. He finished the year at the asylum full of the faith, hope, and joy he would later write about in poetic hymn form.

Cowper began his new life near Cambridge with the Unwin family who took him in as a boarder. Soon, however, Mr. Unwin died, and William was devastated. Providentially, Reverend John Newton, the converted slave ship captain and hymn-writer, came to visit Mrs. Unwin. Having lost his own mother at age seven and then being sent to a severe boarding school by his father, John Newton felt compelled to take the broken William under his pastoral care for rehabilitation.

Another new life began in Olney for William under the tutelage of the godly Newton. The minister interested Cowper in gardening, carpentry, pets of all kinds, birds, and a printing press. Besides working on indoor projects, Newton soon had William conducting village prayer meetings with him, visiting the sick, and distributing donated goods to the poor.

Cowper faithfully attended church, drinking in the heartwarming sermons. He accepted Newton's gracious offer to write together and compose a book of hymns. Every morning the two would meet in the beautiful gardens between William's cottage and Newton's rectory. Surrounded by the sound of the birds they had studied together and the array of wild flowers, the two poets wrote. The result was a collection entitled "Olney Hymns," which provided new hymns for congregational singing. One of William's finest spoke of the providence of God. As he had experienced with every bitter turn in his life, "God Moves in a Mysterious Way."

The tune for "There Is a Fountain Filled with Blood" was an early American melody arranged by a bank clerk from Boston who founded the Boston Academy of Music. Lowell Mason was known to ask poets for a copy of their words or to search through old hymn texts for material. Waiting for the beauty of the words to settle in his mind, he would "find" a melody that was suitable. His mind was quite a vast treasure storehouse since he listened constantly to Handel and other great composers.

Although William Cowper suffered from periodic bouts with depression and a recurring sense of deep guilt and the fear that God could not accept him, he gave us glorious verse and hymns. His ability to listen to God's whispers to his heart gave us the "nobler, sweeter song" as his legacy.

Up from
the Grave
He
Arose

ROBERT LOWRY
1826-1899

Low in the grave he lay—Jesus, my Savior,
Waiting the coming day—Jesus, my Lord.

Refrain:
Up from the grave he arose, with a mighty triumph o'er his foes.
He arose a victor from the dark domain,
And he lives forever with his saints to reign.
He arose! He arose! Hallelujah! Christ arose!

Vainly they watch his bed—Jesus, my Savior;
Vainly they seal the dead—Jesus, my Lord.

Death cannot keep his prey—Jesus my Savior;
He tore the bars away—Jesus, my Lord.

At the Heart of the Hymn

Joni Eareckson Tada

> *It was not possible that he should be holden of [death].*
>
> —ACTS 2:24, KJV

I WAS FAR TOO LITERAL WHEN I WAS A KID.

Like the way I'd read the words to a hymn. Well, maybe not *read*—I was too young to handle the big words in most stanzas. But I was good at memorizing, and with a hymn-singing family like mine, I quickly learned the words to scores of old hymns. And I took those words literally.

Children tend to do that. Whenever I'd come across a mysterious line in a hymn, I'd look for its counterpart in my world. I was amazed the first time I saw an old rugged cross on a hill far away—I wondered if it was the same one Jesus died on. The first time I ever won a trophy in a contest in Brownies, I clutched it happily and tightly in my hands "'til my trophies at last I lay down" on my dresser that night. I was amazed to think heaven might have a judge who handed out trophies.

Then there was that first time I walked in a garden alone while the dew was still on the roses—I was sure God was right behind me as He walked with me and talked with me and told me I was His own.

Once on a cold December night when Daddy and I, with skates slung over our shoulders, went trudging down the snowy streets toward frozen Woodlawn Pond, I was struck with the silent night, holy night; all was calm, all was bright. Straight ahead, directly above the street, a brilliant star glimmered. "Is that the same star that was above Bethlehem?" I asked in all seriousness. Daddy said no, but I wasn't convinced.

Yep, children can be pretty literal. For the most part, it's benign and endearing and, in fact, can tend to excite the imagination, creating wonder and mystery. But there was nothing wonderful about the first time I sang the refrain to "Up from the Grave He Arose."

It was Easter Sunday, somewhere around the mid-fifties. I stood in the pew alongside my three older sisters, all of us wearing straw hats with black velvet hat bands, white gloves, patent leather shoes, and frilly socks. Kathy, Jay and Linda, with hymnals in hand, turned to "Up from the Grave He Arose." I had never sung this one, but always enjoyed learning a new song. The verse began soft, slow, and even sad:

Low in the grave he lay—Jesus my Savior,
Waiting the coming day—Jesus, my Lord.

My sisters seemed to know it. They caught me by surprise, however, when they drew a deep breath right before the refrain. I didn't know where they were going with this one, but followed as best I could as they belted out the chorus with great gusto.

Up from the grave he arose, with a mighty triumph o'er his foes.
He arose a victor from the dark domain,
and he lives forever with his saints to reign.
He arose! He arose! Hallelujah! Christ arose!

Everyone was halfway through the refrain while I was still back on the first six words. *Up from the gravy He arose?* I peered at Kathy's hymnal, trying hard to read the lines (impossible for me, a first grader). I couldn't imagine such a thing. *Why would Jesus be in gravy?* Whenever I heard this hymn, I pictured the Lord buried in brown creamy sauce, the kind Aunt Kitty served with her roast beef. What a weird imagination; that is, until I learned to actually read the refrain. And with reading came understanding.

Funny, the things we think as a child. One friend told me she thought Pontius Pilate was a "conscious pilot." Another used to think that "'round yon virgin" meant that the virgin was not only young, but a little overweight.

It's nothing to be alarmed about, and most kids grow out of it, but it's a good reminder. Boys and girls—and new Christians—need guidance. That's why it's always helpful to take time to open the Word and go step by step and word by word with someone who's young in the faith. "This is what the Word means." "That's why God did thus-and-such." It's not unlike the way "Philip ran up to the chariot and heard the man reading Isaiah the prophet. 'Do you understand what you are reading?' Philip asked. 'How can I,' he said, 'unless someone explains it to me?' So he invited Philip to come up and sit with him" (Acts 8:30-31).

Invite a child to come and sit. Ask, "May I explain this to you?" It's one sure way to keep God out of a gravy boat.

IN THE LIGHT OF THE WORD
John MacArthur

THE MUSIC OF THIS SIMPLE HYMN heightens its emotional impact. The stanzas are sung slowly and somberly, evoking a mood of deep sobriety and sorrow. But the refrain shifts to a quicker tempo and a jubilant melody, joyously heralding the good news of Jesus' triumphant resurrection.

The upbeat tone of the refrain reminds us of the overwhelming joy the disciples must have felt when they finally realized Christ was truly risen from the dead.

During and immediately after the crucifixion, their mood was anything but joyful. Their hopes were dashed. They were ashamed at their own failure

(Matthew 26:56). Everything looked bleak and hopeless. Christ, their beloved Lord, lay "low in the grave."

What they didn't realize was that a great triumph had already been won. When Christ said, "It is finished" and died (John 19:30), He was saying the earthly work He had come to do was complete. Atonement for sin had been made. Satan was defeated. All that remained was for the Son of Man to lie low in the grave for a time, as Jonah had been in the belly of the whale (cf. Matthew 12:40). He was merely "waiting the coming day." Then "up from the grave . . . He arose a victor from the dark domain."

Stanza 2 is a reference to the Romans' vain attempts to guard the body of Jesus. Remember, they had set a guard because the Pharisees recalled Jesus' promise to rise in three days, and they wanted to make sure no one would steal the body and claim He had risen (Matthew 27:63). But there was no way they could actually keep Him from rising. "Death cannot keep his prey."

It is remarkable that although the Pharisees remembered Christ's prophecy about His resurrection, the disciples did not. Their state of mind should not be hard for us to understand. They were discouraged. They no doubt felt partly responsible. It was as if their whole world had suddenly come to an end. They were in a state of deep mourning, mixed with unbearable shame.

Even after Christ arose and appeared to them, the disciples were slow to appreciate the significance of His resurrection. Some of them actually walked with the risen Christ on the road to Emmaus and yet didn't even recognize Him until He finally opened their eyes.

But on the evening of the Resurrection, that changed. The disciples were hiding in fear of the Jewish leaders. They had locked themselves in a room together, where they thought they would be safe. Suddenly, Christ appeared in their midst and said, "Peace be with you!" (John 20:19). Then He "showed them his hands and side" (v. 20)—and they knew for certain that He had truly arisen. Verse 20 says, "The disciples were overjoyed." They now knew He had truly arisen. The rest of their lives was devoted to spreading the message: "He arose! He arose! Hallelujah, Christ arose!"

The resurrection of Christ is one of the most well-attested facts of history. In 1 Corinthians 15:5-8 the apostle Paul recounts all the eyewitnesses—literally hundreds of them—who saw the risen Christ with their own eyes. Those hundreds of eyewitness accounts have never been repudiated. The empty grave was never explained away. And another convincing proof of the Resurrection was the stark transformation of the disciples, who were timid and frightened souls at the time of the crucifixion but within a few weeks' time became fearless preachers of the Gospel. Their ministry ultimately changed the world. That cannot be explained unless they really *did* see Jesus and realize the power of His resurrection. Seeing Christ gave them incredible courage and conviction. They knew beyond a doubt that He had truly arisen. Their Lord had conquered death. "And He lives forever with His saints to reign."

FROM OUT OF THE PAST

Bobbie Wolgemuth

*I*T WAS WITH NO FORMAL TRAINING in musical composition that the American hymn-writer, Robert Lowry, gave us notable gospel favorites such as "Shall We Gather at the River," "Nothing But the Blood," and the Easter hymn "Christ Arose." As a preacher, teacher, and pastor, his passion was God's Word. The music he wrote was a natural gift that flowed from a mind saturated with the Bible and good literature.

Having made a profession of faith in his late teen years, Lowry attended Bucknell University in Pennsylvania, subsequently graduating with honors. He became a professor of literature and later received a doctorate from the university. With the same ability that had enabled him to inspire students, he stirred his parishioners as the pastor of a church near Philadelphia. Confident of his call to ministry, he stayed in the pastorate for the rest of his life, serving several congregations in Pennsylvania, New York, and New Jersey.

Robert's special interest and avocation was music, especially hymnology. He had a favorite pump organ at his home and would sit in the evenings to play and sing. Thoughts that had long been forming in his mind found clear musical expression as he sat in the parlor. Often he would transfer to paper the words and music he heard spinning in his head.

One such night his devotions had centered on the events of the Resurrection. With tender emotion, he mentally stood in astonishment at the empty tomb. His imagination flowing with boldness, he penned "Up from the Grave He Arose," accompanied by a spontaneous, triumphant melody. What a musical proclamation came forth from his parlor that night!

Besides composing music, Robert also compiled songbooks like *Pure Gold* to teach hymns to children in what he called the "quiet revolution" of Sunday school. The ammunition of choice was hymns. He was sold on the converting power of hymns. Children's voices singing words of biblical doctrine and instruction, he felt, would "mould the coming constituents of the Commonwealth." Amazingly, many of the hymns from his collection were taught in public school and for years shaped the youngest American minds.

From the soul and pen of this gifted pastor and musician came choice hymns like "All the Way My Savior Leads Me" and "We're Marching to Zion." His many songbooks and compilations were used in evangelistic crusades in the United States and Great Britain. Although universal notoriety was not his goal, Lowry's special ability to clothe inspiring words with singable tunes enhanced sacred music worldwide.

When I Survey the Wondrous Cross

ISAAC WATTS
1674 - 1748

ARRANGED BY LOWELL MASON
1792 - 1872

When I survey the wondrous cross on which the Prince of glory died,

My richest gain I count but loss, and pour contempt on all my pride.

Forbid it, Lord, that I should boast, save in the death of Christ my God:

All the vain things that charm me most, I sacrifice them to his blood.

See, from his head, his hands, his feet, sorrow and love flow mingled down:

Did e'er such love and sorrow meet, or thorns compose so rich a crown?

Were the whole realm of nature mine, that were a present far too small;

Love so amazing, so divine, demands my soul, my life, my all.

At the Heart of the Hymn
Robert Wolgemuth

May I never boast except in the cross of our Lord Jesus Christ.

—GALATIANS 6:14

HESE ARE MY TOYS." "I GOT AN A." "That's my girlfriend." "What do you think of my diploma?" "Did you hear about my promotion?" "This is my car." "My family." "My portfolio." "My new home." "I'm proud to be an American." "I'm proud of you." "This is mine and I'm proud of it."

This positive attitude may successfully ease our inborn feelings of insecurity and motivate us to do our best. But there is a pride that can be nothing short of hazardous.

Bobbie and I met Father John Powell soon after our wedding in 1970. His kindness and counsel gave us great encouragement at the beginning of our marriage journey. Father John was a Jesuit priest, a tender, godly man brimming with loads of dry wit and wisdom. During the 1970s he was introduced to the world through his brilliant teaching and his insightful books including *Why Am I Afraid to Tell You Who I Am?* and *Why Am I Afraid to Love?* One evening at an interfaith couples' retreat, Father Powell told us a story.

Just a few years out of seminary, John was preparing to lead his small congregation in a special Good Friday worship service. He had prepared a short sermon that he truly hoped would stir them. All alone in a small room just a few feet from the chancel, the young priest was getting ready. His elegant vestments had been freshly dry-cleaned. As he pulled them from the cleaner's plastic, they smelled wonderful. Pure. Perfectly appropriate for this moment.

He slipped into the robes, zipping and hooking them securely. He pulled the colorful stole over his head and adjusted it perfectly. A full-length mirror stood in the corner of the room. Father Powell couldn't help himself. He turned and stood facing the glass, filled with a kind of pious presumption he had never felt before. Not like this.

You are one impressive-looking priest, John silently mused. He turned slowly, keeping his eyes on himself. Having made a complete rotation, the priest took one final look. A smile began to form. After years of seminary, Father Powell had earned this moment. *This is going to be good.*

Through the door, John could hear the organ starting the prelude. The strains of a familiar Good Friday hymn filled his small dressing room like an intoxicating fragrance. He glanced at his watch. It was almost time for Mass to begin. John turned to face the door. He slowly began to move toward it when something caught his eye.

Right above the door was a crucifix—Jesus Christ, hanging on the cross. Unlike the handsome priest's, the Savior's vestments were nothing more than a loincloth. His stole was His nakedness. A crown of thorns was pressed into the flesh of His head. The only color on the image was from His precious blood.

Nothing could have looked more pathetic.

The priest hesitated. Then, as if someone had slapped his face with an open hand, Father Powell was stunned by what he saw, frozen and unable to open the door. In a moment his shock turned to embarrassment, then abject shame. He fell to his knees.

"What am I doing here?" the priest cried aloud, burying his face in his hands.

"Oh, please forgive me, my Holy Father," he wept. "I am not worthy even to kneel in Your holy presence. How could I dare to stand . . . or to speak?"

A few minutes later Father Powell gently opened the door and walked across the open chancel to his seat. Some of the parishioners in the first few pews couldn't help but notice the bleary eyes and slightly wrinkled vestments of their youthful priest. *Perhaps,* they may have thought to themselves, *he didn't have enough time to get ready. He's young. He'll learn.*

What the members of his parish couldn't have known that morning was that a simple glimpse of the cross had not only prepared John for this moment, but had seared a permanent image in his mind of the Crucified One.

It was at this moment that Father John Powell was truly ready to worship.

When I survey the wondrous cross
On which the Prince of Glory died,
My richest gain I count but loss,
And pour contempt on all my pride.

IN THE LIGHT OF THE WORD
John MacArthur

RARELY DO WE COME TO THE LORD'S TABLE in our church without singing this magnificent hymn about the cross. The apostle Paul said, "For whenever you eat this bread and drink this cup, you proclaim the Lord's death until he comes" (1 Corinthians 11:26). Isaac Watts's classic hymn of remembrance seems to capture the very essence of how we as believers ought to remember and regard our Lord's sufferings.

The cross is wondrous, first of all, because it was "the Prince of Glory" who died there. Wicked men with evil intentions put Him to death, but behind the scenes God was sovereignly working to accomplish through Christ's death the greatest good the world has ever seen (Acts 2:23).

How could mere men crucify the Lord of glory? The simple truth is that He went to the cross voluntarily. He said, "I lay down my life. . . . No one takes it from me, but I lay it down of my own accord. I have authority to lay it down and authority to take it up again" (John 10:17-18).

That surely puts human pride in its proper perspective. If the omnipotent Prince of glory would humble Himself and submit to being killed in such a humiliating way for the sake of undeserving sinners, we certainly ought to "pour contempt on all [our] pride."

In that first stanza, Watts echoes the apostle Paul in the words, "My richest gain I count but loss." Paul said, "I consider everything a loss compared to the surpassing greatness of knowing Christ Jesus my Lord, for whose sake I have lost all things. I consider them rubbish, that I may gain Christ" (Philippians 3:8). As Moses knew even in his time, "disgrace for the sake of Christ [is] of greater value than the treasures of Egypt" (Hebrews 11:26).

Stanza 2 is simply a poetic paraphrase of Galatians 6:14: "May I never boast except in the cross of our Lord Jesus Christ, through which the world has been crucified to me, and I to the world."

Stanza 3 vividly describes the paradox of the cross, where "Love and faithfulness meet together; righteousness and peace kiss each other" (Psalm 85:10). Watts borrows the imagery of the blood and water that poured from Christ's side (probably because His pericardium was pierced by the Roman spear that was thrust into Him to insure that He was dead). The hymn invokes that scene as a graphic picture of how "sorrow and love flow mingled down" from the wounds of Christ. "Sorrow" speaks of Christ's grief over humanity's sinfulness; "love" is what moved Him to atone for sinners. Infinite measures of those two passions converged dramatically at the cross in a stark display of the divine attitude toward sin.

Meanwhile, the thorns that were thrust onto Jesus' head in an act of cruel mockery become, in the hymn-writer's view, the richest crown of glory ever worn.

The final stanza acknowledges that no human response can ever be a sufficient expression of gratitude for the infinite mercy and grace that have been bestowed through Christ. If the whole world were ours to give back to Christ, it would be "far too small" a gift. Love of this magnitude demands "my soul, my life, my all."

The famous missionary C. T. Studd gave up wealth, fame, and a career as one of England's leading athletes in order to go to the Congo as a missionary in the late nineteenth century. Asked why he would choose such hardship over a life of comfort, Studd perfectly captured the gist of this hymn's final stanza when he wrote, "If Jesus Christ be God and died for me, no sacrifice can be too great for me to make for Him."

FROM OUT OF THE PAST
Bobbie Wolgemuth

*I*T IS NO WONDER THAT ISAAC WATTS became a brilliant thinker, theologian, and later known as the "father of English hymnody." His parents were passionate about their Christian convictions and emphasized the highest educational standards. From earliest boyhood, Isaac was exposed to religious persecution. He was the ninth child born to a father who was imprisoned three times for dissenting from Anglican Church doctrine. It was said that his mother would visit the jail and sit on a block opposite the cell, nursing baby Isaac while conversing with her husband through the bars.

Isaac learned Latin at age four, Greek at age eight, studied French when he was eleven, and Hebrew when he was thirteen. He had an insatiable appetite for books and especially enjoyed rolling poetry over in his mind as a youngster. At home Isaac constantly spoke in verse, which sometimes annoyed his father.

The precocious boy was once spanked for interrupting evening prayers with a witty verse when he saw a mouse run up the fireplace. "A mouse for want of better stairs, ran up a rope to say his prayers," was met with a stern paternal reprimand. The quick retort from Isaac to his father was, "O father, do some pity take, and I will no more verses make."

His rhyming tendencies were finally turned loose to his father's pleasure when

Isaac was fifteen years old. No longer able to endure the tedious droning of Psalms being lined out and chanted in church services, Isaac decided to compose hymns that could be understood by peasants and children. These hymns speedily found their way into parishioners' hearts. Although completely based on Psalms and Scripture and full of praise to God, his hymns became the object of skeptical scrutiny and dissatisfaction. The established church, which remained stuck in metrical psalming, lost members to the vibrant singing in the dissenting congregations. Familiar with persecution, and zealously endeavoring to use his incredible language skills to write hymns to the level of common understanding, Isaac fearlessly continued writing the objectionable hymns criticized for being "of human composure."

Isaac was loved and admired by an Independent London congregation he served for over twenty years. Frail health in his middle years ended his pastorate, and he spent the remaining years of his life at the country estate of Sir Thomas Abney, a prominent Englishman, and his family. It was here that this man of small stature enjoyed long walks in the elaborate gardens and found an appropriate outdoor sanctuary for writing on a wide range of interests including philosophy, geography, astronomy, psychology, and theology.

Although he never married, Isaac loved children and took an interest in the three Abney daughters. He helped with their moral and religious education and wrote a book for them entitled *Divine and Moral Songs*, which sold hundreds of thousands of copies and became an English classic. Parents all over England encouraged their children with Watts's rhymes to love and serve God.

Isaac set theology to music with hymns like "Jesus Shall Reign," "Joy to the World," "Am I a Soldier of the Cross," and "I Sing the Mighty Power of God." The grandest of all Watts's hymns, "Our God, Our Help in Ages Past," and his most beloved Communion hymn, "When I Survey the Wondrous Cross," are found in hymnals worldwide. The poetic genius of the little man with a big heart for God is his legacy of conviction, passion, and faith.

The Hymns

WORDS AND MUSIC

Christ the Lord Is Risen Today

1. "Christ the Lord is ris'n to-day," Al - - le - lu - ia!
2. Vain the stone, the watch, the seal; Al - - le - lu - ia!
3. Lives a - gain our glo - rious King; Al - - le - lu - ia!
4. Soar we now where Christ has led, Al - - le - lu - ia!

sons of men and an - gels say; Al - - le - lu - ia!
Christ has burst the gates of hell: Al - - le - lu - ia!
where, O death, is now thy sting? Al - - le - lu - ia!
fol - l'wing our ex - alt - ed Head; Al - - le - lu - ia!

raise your joys and tri - umphs high; Al - - le - lu - ia!
death in vain for - bids his rise; Al - - le - lu - ia!
Once he died, our souls to save; Al - - le - lu - ia!
made like him, like him we rise; Al - - le - lu - ia!

sing ye heav'ns, and earth, re - ply. Al - - le - lu - ia!
Christ has o - pened par - a - dise. Al - - le - lu - ia!
where thy vic - to - ry, O grave? Al - - le - lu - ia!
ours the cross, the grave, the skies, Al - - le - lu - ia!

5 Hail, the Lord of earth and heav'n! *Alleluia!*
Praise to thee by both be giv'n; *Alleluia!*
thee we greet triumphant now; *Alleluia!*
hail, the Resurrection, thou! *Alleluia!*

EASTER HYMN 7.7.7.7.al.
Lyra Davidica, 1708; alt.

Charles Wesley, 1739

— 122 —

What Wondrous Love Is This

1. What won-drous love is this, O my soul, O my soul, what
2. To God and to the Lamb, I will sing, I will sing, to
3. And when from death I'm free, I'll sing on, I'll sing on, and

won-drous love is this, O my soul! What won-drous love is
God and to the Lamb, I will sing; to God and to the
when from death I'm free, I'll sing on; and when from death I'm

this that caused the Lord of bliss to bear the dread-ful curse for my
Lamb, who is the great I AM, while mil-lions join the theme, I will
free, I'll sing and joy-ful be, and through e-ter-ni-ty I'll sing

soul, for my soul, to bear the dread-ful curse for my soul!
sing, I will sing, while mil-lions join the theme, I will sing!
on, I'll sing on, and through e-ter-ni-ty I'll sing on!

American folk hymn

WONDROUS LOVE 12.9.12.9.
The Southern Harmony, 1835

Were You There?

1. Were you there when they cru-ci-fied my Lord? (Were you there?)
2. Were you there when they nailed him to the tree? (Were you there?)
3. Were you there when they pierced him in the side? (Were you there?)
4. Were you there when they laid him in the tomb? (Were you there?)
5. Were you there when he rose up from the dead? (Were you there?)

Were you there when they cru-ci-fied my Lord? (Were you there?)
Were you there when they nailed him to the tree? (Were you there?)
Were you there when they pierced him in the side? (Were you there?)
Were you there when they laid him in the tomb? (Were you there?)
Were you there when he rose up from the dead? (Were you there?)

Oh! . . . . Some-times it caus-es me to trem-ble, trem-ble,
(5.) Some-times I feel like shout-ing glo-ry, glo-ry,

trem-ble. Were you there when they cru-ci-fied my Lord? (Were you there?)
trem-ble. Were you there when they nailed him to the tree? (Were you there?)
trem-ble. Were you there when they pierced him in the side? (Were you there?)
trem-ble. Were you there when they laid him in the tomb? (Were you there?)
glo-ry! Were you there when he rose up from the dead? (Were you there?)

Spiritual

WERE YOU THERE? Irreg.
Spiritual

He Was Wounded for Our Transgressions

Thomas O. Chisholm, 1941

OAK PARK Irreg.
Merrill Dunlop, 1941; alt. 1990

Jesus Paid It All

1. I hear the Sav-ior say, "Your strength in-deed is small,
2. Lord, now in-deed I find your power, and yours a-lone,
3. For noth-ing good have I where-by your grace to claim—
4. And when, be-fore the throne, I stand in him com-plete,

child of weak-ness, watch and pray, find in me your all in all."
can change the lep-er's spots, and melt the heart of stone.
I'll wash my gar-ments white in the blood of Cal-v'ry's Lamb.
"Je-sus died my soul to save," my lips shall still re-peat.

REFRAIN

Je - sus paid it all, all to him I owe;

sin had left a crim-son stain, he washed it white as snow.

Elvina M. Hall, 1865; mod.

ALL TO CHRIST 6.6.7.7.ref.
John T. Grape, 1868

Beneath the Cross of Jesus

1. Be - neath the cross of Je - sus I fain would take my stand,
2. Up - on the cross of Je - sus mine eye at times can see
3. I take, O cross, thy shad - ow for my a - bid - ing place:

the shad - ow of a might - y Rock with - in a wea - ry land;
the ver - y dy - ing form of One who suf - fered there for me:
I ask no oth - er sun - shine than the sun - shine of his face;

a home with - in the wil - der - ness, a rest up - on the way,
and from my strick - en heart with tears two won - ders I con - fess,
con - tent to let the world go by, to know no gain nor loss;

from the burn - ing of the noon - tide heat and the bur - den of the day.
the won - ders of re - deem - ing love and my un - wor - thi - ness.
my sin - ful self my on - ly shame, my glo - ry all the cross.

Elizabeth C. Clephane, 1872
Alt. 1990

ST. CHRISTOPHER 7.6.8.6.8.6.8.6.
Frederick C. Maker, 1881

— 127 —

And Can It Be That I Should Gain

1. And can it be that I should gain an in - t'rest
2. 'Tis mys - t'ry all! Th'Im - mor - tal dies: who can ex -
3. He left his Fa - ther's throne a - bove (so free, so
4. Long my im - pris - oned spir - it lay fast bound in
5. No con - dem - na - tion now I dread; Je - sus, and

in the Sav - ior's blood? Died he for me, who caused his
plore his strange de - sign? In vain the first - born ser - aph
in - fi - nite his grace!), hum - bled him - self (so great his
sin and na - ture's night; thine eye dif - fused a quick - 'ning
all in him, is mine! A - live in him, my liv - ing

pain? For me, who him to death pur - sued? A - maz - ing love!
tries to sound the depths of love di - vine. 'Tis mer - cy all!
love!), and bled for all his cho - sen race. 'Tis mer - cy all,
ray; I woke, the dun - geon flamed with light; my chains fell off,
Head, and clothed in righ - teous - ness di - vine, bold I ap - proach

How can it be that thou, my God, shouldst
Let earth a - dore, let an - gel minds in -
im - mense and free; for, O my God, it
my heart was free; I rose, went forth, and
th'e - ter - nal throne, and claim the crown, through

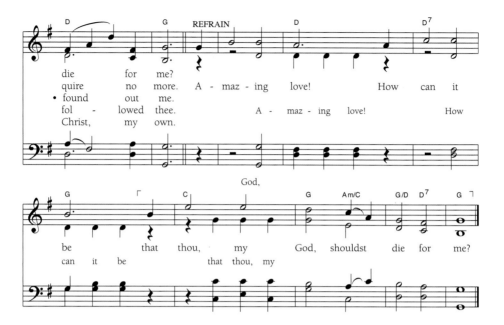

die   for   me?
quire   no   more. A - maz - ing   love!   How   can   it
• found out   me.
fol - lowed thee.   A - maz - ing   love!   How
Christ, my   own.

God,

be   that   thou,   my   God,   shouldst   die   for   me?
can   it   be   that   thou,   my

Charles Wesley, 1738
Alt. 1990

SAGINA L.M.D.
Thomas Campbell, 1825

Jesus, Keep Me Near the Cross

1. Je - sus, keep me near the cross; there a pre - cious foun - tain,
2. Near the cross, a trem - bling soul, love and mer - cy found me;
3. Near the cross! O Lamb of God, bring its scenes be - fore me;
4. Near the cross I'll watch and wait, hop - ing, trust - ing ev - er,

free to all — a heal - ing stream — flows from Cal - v'ry's moun - tain.
there the Bright and Morn - ing Star shed its beams a - round me.
help me walk from day to day with its sha - dow o'er me.
till I reach the gold - en strand just be - yond the riv - er.

REFRAIN

In the cross, in the cross, be my glo - ry ev - er;

till my rap - tured soul shall find rest be - yond the riv - er.

Fanny J. Crosby, 1869

NEAR THE CROSS 7.6.7.6.ref.
William H. Doane, 1869

There Is a Fountain Filled with Blood

1. There is a foun-tain filled with blood, drawn from Im-man-uel's veins;
2. The dy-ing thief re-joiced to see that foun-tain in his day;
3. E'er since by faith I saw the stream your flow-ing wounds sup-ply,
4. Then in a no-bler, sweet-er song I'll sing your pow'r to save,
5. Dear dy-ing Lamb, your pre-cious blood shall nev-er lose its pow'r,

and sin-ners, plunged be-neath that flood, lose all their guilt-y stains:
and there have I, as vile as he, washed all my sins a-way:
• re-deem-ing love has been my theme, and shall be till I die:
when this poor lisp-ing, stam-m'ring tongue lies si-lent in the grave:
till all the ran-somed church of God be saved to sin no more:

lose all their guilt-y stains, lose all their guilt-y stains;
washed all my sins a-way, washed all my sins a-way;
• and shall be till I die, and shall be till I die;
lies si-lent in the grave, lies si-lent in the grave;
be saved to sin no more, be saved to sin no more;

and sin-ners, plunged be-neath that flood, lose all their guilt-y stains.
and there have I, as vile as he, washed all my sins a-way.
• re-deem-ing love has been my theme, and shall be till I die.
when this poor lisp-ing, stam-m'ring tongue lies si-lent in the grave.
till all the ran-somed church of God be saved to sin no more.

William Cowper, 1771
Mod.

FOUNTAIN 8.6.8.6.6.6.8.6.
Lowell Mason, 1830

— 131 —

Up from the Grave He Arose

He a-rose a victor from the dark do-main, and he
lives for-ev-er with his saints to reign. He a-rose!
He a-rose!
He a-rose! Hal-le-lu-jah! Christ a-rose!
He a-rose!

Robert Lowry, 1874

CHRIST AROSE 11.10.ref.
Robert Lowry, 1874

When I Survey the Wondrous Cross

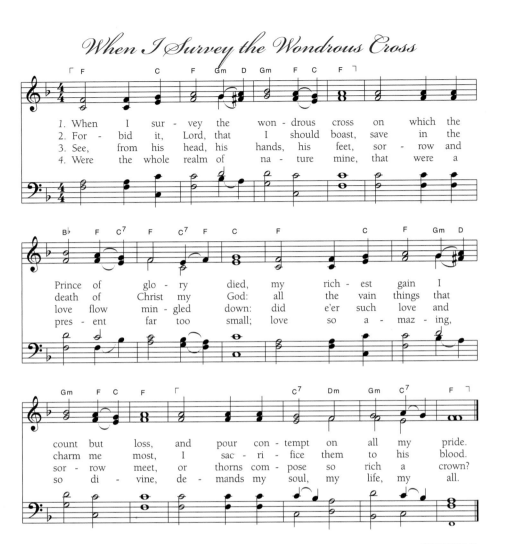

1. When I sur-vey the won-drous cross on which the
2. For-bid it, Lord, that I should boast, save in the
3. See, from his head, his hands, his feet, sor-row and
4. Were the whole realm of na-ture mine, that were a

Prince of glo-ry died, my rich-est gain I
death of Christ my God: all the vain things that
love flow min-gled down: did e'er such love and
pres-ent far too small; love so a-maz-ing,

count but loss, and pour con-tempt on all my pride.
charm me most, I sac-ri-fice them to his blood.
sor-row meet, or thorns com-pose so rich a crown?
so di-vine, de-mands my soul, my life, my all.

Isaac Watts, 1707, 1709

HAMBURG L.M.
Gregorian chant
Arr. by Lowell Mason, 1824

Jesus, Thy Blood and Righteousness

1. Je - sus, thy blood and righ - teous - ness my beau - ty
2. Bold shall I stand in thy great day; for who aught
3. When from the dust of death I rise to claim my
4. Je - sus, be end - less praise to thee, whose bound - less
5. O let the dead now hear thy voice; now bid thy

are, my glo - rious dress; 'midst flam - ing worlds, in
to my charge shall lay? Ful - ly ab - solved through
man - sion in the skies, ev'n then this shall be
mer - cy hath for me— for me a full a -
ban - ished ones re - joice; their beau - ty this, their

these ar - rayed, with joy shall I lift up my head.
these I am from sin and fear, from guilt and shame.
all my plea, Je - sus hath lived, hath died, for me.
tone - ment made, an ev - er - last - ing ran - som paid.
glo - rious dress, Je - sus, thy blood and righ - teous - ness.

Nikolaus Ludwig von Zinzendorf, 1739
Tr. by John Wesley, 1740; alt.

GERMANY L.M.
William Gardiner's *Sacred Melodies*, 1815